Prob... ution

B...

In... ...s and ...amilies

Re... ...ded ...ion

Eva... ...son and **Harvey Ratner**

BT Press

First Edition Published May 1990

Revised and expanded Second Edition Published September 1999

Published by Brief Therapy Press
17 Avenue Mansions, Finchley Road, London NW3 7AX

© Evan George, Chris Iveson and Harvey Ratner, 1990 & 1999

Designed by Alex Gollner

ISBN 1 871697 65 4

CONTENTS

THE AUTHORS

Evan George, Chris Iveson and Harvey Ratner are the co-founders of the Brief Therapy Practice. The Practice is a training, consulting and clinical organisation based in London. Established in 1989 it now offers Europe's largest training programme in solution focused brief therapy.

The core (and passionate) interest of the authors remains the development of solution focused thinking and its flexible application in the widest range of contexts.

Members of The Brief Therapy Practice:

Yasmin Ajmal	Evan George
Chris Iveson	Diana Iveson
Jane Lethem	Harvey Ratner

Brief Therapy Practice
4d Shirland Mews
London W9 3DY
Tel: (020) 8968 0070
Fax: (020) 8964 4192
Brief3@aol.com

FOREWORD TO THE FIRST EDITION

By Steve de Shazer

I have a confession to make: When I first was given this book, I was curious and I started reading it with interest until I got to the table of contents which quickly sent me into Chapter One where, upon seeing the top of page 2, I quit. I then procrastinated, postponing my reading of it as long as I possibly could. I prolonged this procrastination until it was no longer viable, i.e., I might get caught out.

Frankly, I was afraid that Evan George, Chris Iveson and Harvey Ratner, whom I had just met briefly, had developed a 'readers' digest' version or a 'cook book' or (my worst nightmare) a statement, a manifesto about the right way to do brief therapy. Perhaps surprisingly, I did not worry about whether or not they had 'understood' my work and the work of my colleagues. After all, even a misunderstanding might turn out to be clinically useful.

Nagged and cajoled finally into reading PROBLEM TO SOLUTION, I was amazed to find evidence in Chapter One that they had gotten the idea. And, in Chapter Two (and subsequent chapters), I saw that not only had they got the idea, but they were able to use it to work with their clients in a useful way. I found Chapter Three (*now Chapter Four*) involved the kind of situation (therapist/team with a statutory case) that many therapists find 'difficult'. But they were not put off stride; they did not pull a Lestrade and chase after red-herrings. Instead, they listened to the client, found out what she wanted and worked with her toward getting it. This is, of course, the core of solution focused brief therapy.

So, I find that I can recommend this book; particularly to busy therapists who do not have the luxury of time and for those therapists who want a place to start exploring solution focused brief therapy. It is not a pastiche, not just a re-packaging of my work. Rather, it is an original contribution: PROBLEM TO SOLUTION can stand on its own two feet.

INTRODUCTION

This book describes an approach to counselling and consultation known as Solution Focused Brief Therapy. It was developed by Steve de Shazer, Insoo Kim Berg and their colleagues at the Brief Family Therapy Center in Milwaukee in the early 1980s.

Its first known use in the UK was by the authors while working together as a team in an NHS child, family and adult psychiatric clinic in central London. In 1990 the first edition of this book was published; it described the approach as it was viewed at the time and included a number of case descriptions to illustrate its application.

It is now almost ten years since the first edition. In that time the authors have developed the Brief Therapy Practice (an independent therapy, training and consultation organisation) into the first solution focused brief therapy centre in the UK and it is now the biggest provider of solution focused brief therapy training in Europe. More significantly, during this time solution focused brief therapy has moved from the margins of professional practice to a much more central position, having become the approach of first resort in many agencies.

Solution Focused Brief Therapy has altered in many significant ways since the first edition was published. Gale Miller, a sociologist who observed the Milwaukee clinic's progress over a 13-year period, has gone so far as to describe two complete stages in the development of the approach (Miller, 1997), and in his terms the approach described in our first edition would be fairly representative of what he calls the first stage. We are less inclined to see the development of the approach as clearly definable 'stages' in the way he sees it; for us it has been a gradual expansion of the model with different elements of the original approach being emphasised in different ways.

Our aim in publishing a revised edition of the book is to take stock of the changes in our own 'version' of solution focused brief therapy. We are more than happy to reproduce the clinical case chapters from the first edition. These were cases seen at the Marlborough Family Service (the NHS 'clinic' of the text) where the authors were working at the time. Our approach has altered over the years, but what is being illustrated in these chapters is in many ways the bedrock of all solution focused practice.

For this new edition we have substantially re-written the first chapter so that the model we are describing reflects what we practice and teach today. We then add a further chapter which specifically details the changes in thinking and practice that we can identify as we look back over the last decade. Then after the four original case chapters, we have added a further one centred on work we have done in the last two years in a mixed comprehensive school in central London. The chapter 'Other Clinical Applications' incorporates material from the first edition and is much expanded. As before, clients' names and some details have been changed to protect their confidentiality.

Finally, there are appendices relating to research findings and further reading. Solution Focused Brief Therapy was a new phenomenon in the field of counselling when we first wrote about it; today it has aged sufficiently for us to review the growing body of research that is evidence of the effectiveness of the approach and therefore, we believe, an endorsement of our original enthusiasm and desire to 'spread the word'.

The chapter on the project in the school is only used as an example of our current practice. We see a mixture of clients, some self-referred and fee paying, others referred through social services, education departments, hospitals and so on. We are also engaged in other projects in the community, such as work with the duty team of a local authority's children and families department where we have used solution focused brief therapy to help prevent the need for young people to be accommodated away from home in times of crisis. We have always seen it as essential to look at ways to bring solution focused thinking into situations where the workers concerned are not working as 'pure' therapists, for example, in statutory contexts. We will continue to expand our use of the approach and thereby hope to contribute to its development and application in the 'difficult' areas that Steve de Shazer refers to in his foreword to the first edition.

CHAPTER ONE

A CO-OPERATIVE THERAPY

FROM PROBLEMS AS RULES
TO EXCEPTIONS AS SOLUTIONS

A simple example from de Shazer's writing illustrates the essence of the solution focused approach. He describes a client who stated that his problem was that he was always depressed. Asked then how he knew he was depressed (because, if he was always depressed, then that would be 'normal' to him), he said that there were times when he felt less depressed. These occasions were, for him, the exceptions that proved the rule, of always being depressed. de Shazer then focused on what the client was doing when he felt less depressed. Problems and the behaviours associated with them are often seen by clients as static situations in which the 'same damn thing' keeps happening: the same damn thing appears to take on the quality of a rule of life. What happens in the client's life when the problem isn't happening (when, for example, he feels less depressed) can therefore be called not 'the exception that proves the rule' but 'the exception to the rule'. It is these exceptions that can then be used to construct solution behaviours: the exceptions themselves forming the basis of the solution, so that clients may only need to do more of what they are already doing in order to solve the problem.

What de Shazer discovered was that by amplifying the 'solution' pattern of behaviours, they began to outweigh the problem patterns. The depressed client did more and more of the things that he did when he was less depressed, and consequently he experienced himself as being less and less depressed. It is as if solution behaviours and thoughts are discontinuous or mutually exclusive to problem behaviours and thoughts.

Brief therapists have for a long time pointed out the importance of a client 'doing something different' because, from a systemic point of view, if one significant person in a system begins to change, the rest of the system will have to change in relation to that person, and, therefore, only a small change may be necessary to set the ball rolling.

However, if in most cases clients like the depressed man are already performing solution behaviours, why do these not have an effect? How is it that the very things that are dismissed at one moment as being the exceptions that *prove* the rule can later become the exceptions that undermine the rule.

Change, it is argued, can arise from either a difference in how a person views his or her world or by a person doing something different, or both. It is obvious that our behaviour is influenced by our beliefs, themselves the result of family and wider social experiences over time. It is also obvious that our beliefs are changed by our experience. If someone dislikes traffic wardens then experiencing a traffic warden as helpful one day might either be seen as the exception which proves the rule or as new evidence which will alter that belief. Why that particular warden on that particular day will make a difference to our previous beliefs and behaviour is a difficult question. So the man who is depressed doesn't see his solution behaviours as being solutions – he believes they simply emphasise the extent of his problem ('prove the rule'). But once the therapist describes them as successes ('exceptions to the rule') the client may start to see his world differently; or, if the client starts to do more of what he is saying is good for him, he may come to believe that he does indeed hold the key to his own solution. The therapeutic endeavour is a search for solutions. A person may need to meet several helpful traffic wardens before changing his or her view of them, just as the therapist needs to help the client identify as many thoughts, feelings and behaviours that are different from the usual, so that they actually start to make a difference.

An important concept in solution focused therapy, based on the Buddhist idea of the illusion of stability, is that change is happening all the time. For clients who feel dominated by a problem that won't go away this is a hard idea to grasp: for them, it is as if time has stood still. But it is an idea that maintains the therapist's optimism for the future, and it has often been said that a function of any therapist is to be a source of hope to clients.

THE TASK OF THE THERAPIST

The consequence of the search for solutions, for the 'difference that will make a difference' (Bateson, 1972), is that in a typical solution-focused interview there is minimal focus on problems: problem-free and solution talk is encouraged wherever possible to enable clients to reach a position of belief in their ability to change their lives.

It is, then, the responsibility of the therapist to guide the conversations in the session towards solution talk. As Ben Furman says, he or she acts as 'Head Solution Talker', creating a way of talking that is more likely to lead to change.

According to Hoffman, the therapist comes into the family 'without any definition of pathology, without any idea about what dysfunctional structures to look for, and without any set idea about what should or should not change' (Hoffman, 1990). The task of the therapist is to join with the family to co-evolve a therapist-family system through which change can occur. The notion of co-evolution derives from second-order cybernetics, in which the observing system of therapist plus team is included in any description of what is thought to be happening in the family, to make it clear that the family is not some objective entity to be acted upon in the therapy situation (first order cybernetics). According to Cecchin (Cecchin, 1987), the stance the therapist needs to take is that of being curious about the family's beliefs and behaviours. The therapist's curiosity is conveyed to the family, who in turn develop a curiosity about alternative descriptions or readings of their story, and consequently can develop new ideas or behaviours. A solution focused therapist has a more explicit interest in change than Cecchin or Hoffman and, as an advocate for change, will focus on solution as a deliberate act to guide the family towards changing. However, it is not an authoritarian act on the part of the therapist: he or she believes change will come about, but is not telling the family *how* to change; he or she merely 'flags' what appear to be solution thoughts and behaviours because the family, while thinking 'problem' (and perhaps encouraged to do so by other professionals and friends), is unable to notice the significance of the exceptions.

SOLUTION TALK

The primary activity of the solution focused brief therapist is, as in most therapies, to ask questions. The particular types of questions belong to two main categories: future-oriented questions that look to identify how the client will know that their problem has been solved, and present- and past-oriented questions that seek to locate successes in the present and the past that are signs of the client's ability to solve their problems.

Examples of future-oriented questions might be:

How will you know things are better? What will you be doing differently then?

If you two weren't arguing so much in future, how would you know that it's not just temporary but that it will last?

How would your son know that you are not letting drink get in the way of your relationship with him?

> When you are less depressed, what is your partner going to see you doing differently?

The last two questions incorporate a technique derived from family therapy, that of engaging a person in speculating as to what the perspective of a significant other might be. These 'other person perspective' questions help a client to see themselves through the eyes of someone who knows them, and thus to develop a richer description of their possibilities.

Examples of past-oriented questions that explore possible successes are:

> What did you do that was good for you in the last week?
>
> How did you do that?
>
> What did your mother see you doing?

We have found that the work of Michael White is rich in change-oriented questions, for example (White and Epston, 1990):

> Can you recall an occasion when you could have given in to the problem but didn't?
>
> What do you think your sister could have noticed about how your relationship coped on this occasion that could have been surprising to her?
>
> What does this change tell you (or me) about you as a person?

THE STAGES OF THERAPY: THE FIRST SESSION

'The purpose of the first session is to establish rapport between client and therapist, focus the client positively toward solution, and establish goals' (Lipchik and de Shazer, 1986).

de Shazer and his colleagues have developed a number of steps to successful therapy, all of which are likely to be taken in the first session. The first session then is a blueprint for the entire therapy and, in our version, consists of six basic areas for exploration with the client:

1. 'Problem-free' talk: building rapport and locating strengths.
2. What the client wants to achieve from the session or the therapy as a whole.
3. A description of a future without the problem.
4. Exceptions: what the client is already doing to move towards their preferred future, and how they are coping.
5. Scales: evaluating the degree of progress already made and

identifying future signs of progress.

6. Constructive feedback regarding the client's skills; offering a suggestion (usually that they observe signs of progress).

This is, of course, a rather thin account of what the therapist will focus on in a typical first session. It by no means does justice to the extent of the therapist's activities. For example, although the session ends with the worker giving the client feedback, they will most likely have taken a short break from the session in order to think about what feedback to give. Furthermore, constructive comments are not reserved only to be given at the end of a session: throughout every solution focused meeting the worker will be searching for and highlighting the client's strengths and resources, and consequently the giving of compliments is a constant theme.

Problem-free talk

Many counselling approaches will begin with a rapport-building 'getting to know you' phase. In solution focused therapy we are specifically interested in successful areas of clients' lives, at home, work, school and elsewhere. This enquiry usually lasts no longer than five minutes, but it enables the worker to convey an interest in the client as a *person* rather than as a walking problem.

Preferred outcome to the session

The 'getting down to business' part of the work begins with asking the client what they hope they might gain from attending the session:

What are your best hopes for this meeting?

Let's say this session turns out to be useful to you. How will you know?

In most cases the client's first response will be a statement of the problem that has brought them to therapy. The therapist will listen respectfully to this, and acknowledge the trouble it is causing the client. But the therapist will avoid asking detailed questions about the problem, moving instead, as quickly as possible, to checking again what the client's preferred outcome would be.

It sounds like it's been very tough for you lately. So, in coming here today, how will you know that this meeting will have made a difference for you?

Sometimes a client will say that what they are hoping for is 'advice' on what to do. In solution focused therapy we seek to avoid giving advice, at least in a way that would seem to impose solutions from an expert position. Our aim will be, ultimately, to elicit from the client their way of doing things well so that we can then 'advise' them to do more of it in future. Nevertheless, it is important that the client's wishes are taken seriously:

> If you leave here today feeling that you received good advice, how will you know? What will you be doing differently then?

If the client remains unclear about what they are hoping to get from the session, it may be because they have been sent; this is particularly likely to be the case in statutory situations.

> What do you think that those who are most concerned about you are hoping that you will get from coming here today? What will they see you doing that will tell them it's been useful?

The worker will ask as many questions as necessary about this in order to establish that there is a positive outcome to the session that the *client* wants – even if that is only to do just enough to get others off their backs!

A future when the problem is solved

There are a variety of questions that workers can draw on to help clients clarify the future they hope to have when the problem is solved. The one most used by solution focused therapists is known as the 'Miracle Question':

de Shazer: So, I have a somewhat strange question, but, uh, suppose that ah… when you go home tonight and you go to bed and you go to sleep, a miracle happens. OK? And the problem that brings you in here is solved.

Client: Mm hm.

dS But you can't know it.

C Mm hm.

dS 'cause it happens while you are sleeping.

C OK.

dS OK?

C All right.

dS So, when you wake up tomorrow morning, what will you notice, what will give you the clues that maybe a miracle has happened? (de Shazer, 1994)

The therapist will seek to draw out the client's vision of the future in as much small, concrete detail as possible. Many clients will answer in terms of feelings they hope to have, and will refer to problem behaviours they hope will have ceased. The solution focused worker will encourage the client to translate feeling statements into behavioural expressions, and will focus on positive descriptions of what the client will be doing, rather than what they will not be doing:

So, when you are feeling happier, what will you be doing then?
After the miracle has happened and you and your partner are arguing less, what will you be doing instead?

The perspective of significant others will be invoked to aid this process of clarification:

What will your partner (or child, or social worker, etc.) see you doing so that they will know a miracle has happened?

Exceptions

With a picture of the preferred future drawn as carefully as possible, it is a simple step to enquire when, in the recent past, aspects, however small, of the miracle scenario have already been happening. In fact, in a large majority of cases clients will spontaneously elicit such memories themselves in the course of describing their preferred future. Again, the worker will aim to draw out as much behavioural detail as possible:

What are the signs, however small, that this miracle is already starting to happen?
When was the last time you were able to ...? (Here, a specific behaviour will be referred to). How did you do that?
If your partner was here now, when would they say was the last time you managed to do that? What would they say they saw you do?

Those positive behaviours that the client says are already happening now are evidence of what the Milwaukee team referred to as 'pre-treatment change' (Weiner-Davis et al, 1987). They developed the idea of inviting the client, for example during the initial telephone call or in the letter offering the appointment, to observe any changes or differences prior to the first session. They found that a significant number of clients then report changes that, of course, can be ascribed to the client's own resources rather than to the effect of therapy. Being able to locate change outside the therapy sessions is a constant goal of the therapist.

Where the client reports few or no positive developments, the worker will enquire how the client has managed to *cope* with life and how they have managed to stop things from getting worse. Again, the aim will be to draw out as much specific detail as possible.

In general, just as the more clearly the client is able to describe their preferred future, the more likely it is that they will want to make the effort to achieve it; so, the more exceptions there are to a problem the quicker a solution will be found.

Scale questions

The practitioner is now in a position to assess with the client the degree of progress already made towards the realisation of their preferred future. There are many ways to use scale questions to this effect, but a typical method is as follows:

> Let us say that 10 represents the day after the miracle has happened and 0 the worst things could possibly be. Where, between 0 and 10, would you say you are right now?

In some of the cases described in this book, a reverse scale of 0 representing the time when the problem is totally solved and 10 representing the time when things were at their worst is used instead.

There are many possible benefits arising from the use of these questions. They are, firstly, a simple means to *assess* progress from session to session. They can be used to ask someone where on the scale they would feel would be 'good enough' for them: frequently this is put at 7 or 8, and therefore the work can terminate at that point. Secondly, in initial sessions it is not uncommon for clients to have an all or nothing attitude: either they are to be totally dominated by the problem ('it always/never happens that ...') or they want the miracle to happen and they want it now! The scale shows them that, generally, life is on a continuum. The average initial session rating is about 3. This enables the worker to enquire how come they are at 3 and not at 0: this leads to the detailing of *exceptions* that are already happening in the client's life. Thereafter, the client can be asked how they will know they have reached *one step* up on the scale, to 4 in this example. The therapist will emphasise that what is being asked for is a description of a *small* step; if fitting, clients can be asked about half points!

Any number of scales can be used. A common example, after assessing a client's general progress towards their preferred future, is to ask what their *confidence* is:

> If 10 represents your total confidence that you will reach the 'good enough' point on the scale, and 0 represents that you don't think there's any chance, where, between 0 and 10, would you say your confidence is right now? How come? What will need to be different for your confidence to be one point higher?

Clients can be asked where on the scales they think significant others would place them; if those others are present they can be asked their views, and it is usually the case that concerned others (parents, partners, etc.) will rate the client's progress slightly higher than the client rates themselves.

In a typical first session, scale questions will represent the last part of actual interviewing.

The 'break': working out what feedback to give

All solution focused sessions will end with constructive feedback to the client and possibly the suggestion of something the client might do or, more usually, look out for after the session. The feedback does not need to take long but the choice of words is very important and therefore a break from the session can give the worker the opportunity to plan what they are going to say. If circumstances allow, the therapist will leave the room to do this.

Compliments flow naturally from a consideration of clients' strengths, and are therefore shared with the client throughout the session. The final feedback may need to be no more than a summary or repetition of compliments already given. Attention is paid to using the client's own words to describe their qualities: the more the client hears things described in their terms the more likely it is that they will feel not only that the therapist has listened carefully to them but also that he or she is not patronising them.

Feedback and suggestion

The session ends with the worker sharing their views with the client. Attention is paid to the client's responses as the feedback is given, so that the therapist can evaluate if the client believes they have been heard correctly: nods of the head are a good sign!

The client is then asked if they want to have a further session. If the answer is 'yes' they are asked when they would like to come back: in general, a longer rather than a shorter gap is preferred so that the client has more time to make and notice changes.

If a suggestion is offered to the client it is usually that the client continue the process begun in the session of looking out for changes and progress:

Notice any improvements
Notice what you are doing as you move up the scale
Notice what you are doing to resist the urge to drink to excess (or

gamble, be violent, steal, argue with the teacher, etc.)

In some situations it is possible to suggest something for the client to do. At its simplest this could be merely to invite the client to do more of what they have learned works best for them in moving them forward. There are a number of more complicated suggestions that can be made; in general the worker should be wary of being too directive, in case the client 'forgets' to do what they've been told and the client-therapist rapport suffers. Some examples of different 'tasks' will be found in the cases discussed in later chapters.

SECOND AND SUBSEQUENT SESSIONS

'The purpose of each successive session is to assess change and to help maintain it so that a solution can be achieved.' (Lipchik and de Shazer, 1986).

On the basis of the belief that change is happening all the time, it is logical that the first question of every subsequent session should be, 'So, what's better?' This begins an enquiry into the very smallest signs of progress that the client has made since the previous session. There is rarely the need to revisit future-focused questions such as the miracle question: it is assumed that if the work of the first session, in clarifying the client's preferred future, has been thorough enough, then subsequent sessions are in essence follow-up on progress towards the preferred future (unless the client has changed their goal). The emphasis, therefore, is on exception questions that assess current progress and identify what the signs of future progress might look like.

The range of solution focused questions referred to previously are drawn upon in order to achieve as full a description as possible. The aim is, again, to have a description that is rich in small, concrete behavioural detail, and 'other person perspective' questions are used to aid this process. Other aspects of the interview process are the same as in the first session, for example the use of a 'think break', the feedback of compliments and, sometimes, the offering of a suggestion.

As with de Shazer, we space our sessions entirely according to how change is progressing, so that generally sessions get further and further apart. We don't believe that we need frequent sessions to urge change along; we want to communicate our belief in the *client's* ability to change things, that change is under their control, not ours.

Sometimes a client will report changes, but will describe them as having arisen *spontaneously* – 'I don't know why, but I've just felt happier recently; maybe I've been sleeping better, but I can't think why that is' or they attribute the changes to other persons or other circumstances – 'it must be the improvement in the weather' or 'I don't know why my son has improved since we were last here, as I've done nothing different; perhaps he's starting to grow up at last!' We would aim to help the client identify at least some small sign of something they themselves did to contribute to the change happening (or at least the possibility that it might happen), so that we arrive at a *deliberate* action they took that is repeatable in the future. If this is not possible – and it is important, of course, not to try to convince the client that they 'really' did do something different if they say they didn't – then they are asked how they *responded* to the change. For example, the parent may feel that they did nothing that led to their child changing his or her behaviour, but they might see that their show of warmth at the change itself encouraged the child to maintain progress in future. The person who feels better as a result of having had a better night's sleep is encouraged to explore the differences in their behaviour (in their eyes and the eyes of others) so that, possibly, they might identify steps they have taken that could be open to them even if they start having difficult nights again.

If clients report no change or even that things are worse, we would acknowledge the feeling of disappointment or frustration that the client might be feeling, but we would also seek to search for exceptions on the assumption that the client's statement that there have been no changes can be heard as 'I haven't *seen* any changes', meaning that there could have *been* changes that the client has difficulty recalling now, maybe because things have got worse in the days immediately before the session. The worker would therefore encourage the client to explore in close detail the time since the last session : sometimes it is found that the first day or two after the last session were better, but the client is now preoccupied with the difficulties of the last few days, and so they would be asked to talk about differences in the earlier days. A further reason why the client may have missed any signs of progress is precisely because there were changes, and this has raised their expectation of what can be achieved – and made them less tolerant of things than they were before. The client may, in effect, be complaining of a different problem, for which a different or broader goal is required. An example is a mother who initially came because her four-year-old daughter was screaming so much she not only disturbed the neighbours but had had to be withdrawn from her playgroup. The mother came to a later session saying things were worse. On closer examination the child was found to have screamed on only one occasion since the last session, but the mother now found her disobedience to be unbearable. This indicates the value of obtaining concrete information in the first session regarding life without the problem.

Finally, if things really have not improved, or have become worse, it could be useful to explore how the client has been *coping* with life, how they continue to survive and how they are managing to stop things becoming even worse. It would also be relevant to check what the client is hoping to gain from the session this time. If things are worse, yet the client has still come for their appointment (or opened their door to you), then it is reasonable to clarify their preferred outcome on this – and perhaps every – occasion. The client may have a different goal; lack of progress since last time may have persuaded them to change their idea of what is now achievable in their lives.

A NOTE ON THE WORD 'BRIEF'

Sometimes clients ask how many sessions we think they will need to solve their problem. We always answer that we treat every session as if it could be the last, because although our average – and that of most brief therapists – is three to four sessions, it is almost impossible to predict who will need one session and who will need ten. de Shazer has found that most clients who scale themselves at a 5 in the first session – not a 4, and not a 6, but a 5! – are likely to need just one session; we feel more research is needed to verify and explain this strange phenomenon!

There is growing evidence (see Miller et al, 1997) that most clients attend therapy for less than ten sessions, regardless of the model of therapy. As proposed in the appendix on research findings, while this might suggest that the choice of model of therapy to use is irrelevant, we would maintain that to choose an approach that is brief by design rather than by default, means that we are focusing on what research tells us clients value most: counselling where what *they* want is attended to and listened to. By these means we can, in de Shazer's words, engage in a therapy which will take 'as few sessions as possible – and not one session longer.'

CHAPTER TWO

TEN YEARS ON

The literature on solution focused brief therapy has grown dramatically since *Problem to Solution* was originally published and it is a testament to the integrity of its basic principles that the approach remains essentially as it was. Solution focused therapists' two principal activities are to find out where clients want to get to, and to discover what they are already doing to get there. However, as more therapists from other models move towards a solution focused approach they bring with them different interpretations of the basic principles of solution focused brief therapy and additions to its techniques. Yvonne Dolan (1991,1998), who has transformed ideas and practices around work with survivors, maintains her links with Ericksonian hypnosis; Bill O'Hanlon, (O'Hanlon and Weiner Davies, 1989; O'Hanlon and Beadle, 1996) also influenced by Erickson (O'Hanlon and Hexum, 1990) continues to add to his 'Possibility Therapy' by including ideas and practices from the Australian 'narrative therapist', Michael White (White and Epston, 1990; White, 1991); the British author, Bill O'Connell (1998), brings a wealth of influence from person-centred and other counselling approaches; and in another British publication, Dave Hawkes, Ian Marsh and Ron Wilgosh (1998) bring a 'post-modern, constructionist' influence to bear in the practice of solution focused therapy in the mental health field. These influences and expansions serve to enrich and extend the model, and to some of these developments, no doubt, will be traced the origins of new models.

Our work has also changed, subject as it is to the constant influence of those we teach, our own reading, discussions, clinical practice and supervision. It is unlikely that our work is any more effective, or that our current way of thinking about it is an improvement on how we thought about it ten years ago, but it is different. We see the changes we have made and are making as necessary to continued interest, if only because, to quote Thom Gunn: 'One is always nearer by not keeping still.'[1]

A PARTING OF THE WAYS?

Our progress has not been in isolation, and of the two main strands of solution focused therapy's development, we are placed very clearly on

---

[1] "On the Move" in Thom Gunn (1994) *Collected Poems*. Farrar Straus & Giroux

one side. Eight years ago we were still wedded to the notion that tasks
were important in brief therapy: we thought that part of the therapist's
job was to assess the client's likelihood of completing a task and the type
of tasks different clients might do. This has remained an important
feature of Steve de Shazer's work and is taken even further by Matthew
Selekman (1993, 1997) in his work with children and adolescents. We
have gone down a different path and have almost dropped tasks from
our repertoire of techniques. But it does have to be said that there are
some exceptions to this rule, especially after Steve de Shazer has made
one of his visits! These two strands were identified by a teenage client
who, as the therapist was leaving for the break, asked: 'How does this
work? Have you been collecting information so you can make an
assessment and tell us what to do, or is it just the process of the
questions and answers?' While de Shazer's work reflects an ability to
include both these aspects to a point where process and task seem almost
indistinguishable, others, like Selekman, are clearly beginning to take
more of an 'expert' position in relation to their clients. As the task
becomes more important, the therapist's thoughts, views and actions
become more dominant. This does not make for poor therapy but it will
eventually lead to a level of difference that will not be confinable within a
single model. Gale Miller (1997), a research sociologist, for many years
associated with de Shazer, Berg and colleagues, provides a fascinating
account of these developments and where they might lead.

Our own shift from task to process took a number of twists and turns
and this chapter gives an account of what, at this time, seem the most
significant.

EVERY CLIENT IS A CUSTOMER, MOTIVATION IS NEVER AN ISSUE

One of Steve de Shazer's early ideas was the categorisation of clients into
customers, complainants and visitors. This implied a theory of
motivation and a way of 'knowing' some hidden client quality. The
follow-up study of our own work, and studies elsewhere show these
distinctions to have little or no predictive value. Given that they tell us
nothing useful, the classification, according to Ockham's principle,
quoted by de Shazer (1985), should be dropped. Neither do outcome
studies (Iveson, 1991; DeJong and Hopwood, 1996) show marked
differences between voluntary and enforced clients which means
assumptions about differences in motivation need to be questioned. Like
de Shazer, in recent years we have adopted the assumption that *all*

clients are motivated for *something*. What we assume is that if, under any circumstances, a client has agreed to speak with us then they are doing so for a good reason, and one connected with our professional role. If we believe otherwise then we are acting on an assumption about the client which is potentially offensive: that they do things without a good reason. Not a good start to what should be a working relationship!

This is not to say that the client is always ready to articulate why they have come. Part of the therapist's task is to ask questions which help clients find a way of expressing to themselves what it is that they actually want.

Therapist: So what are your hopes for this session?

Client: I don't know, I really don't know why I'm here.

T So how come you decided to come?

C I don't know, it was just that the doctor said you wanted to see me.

T So if seeing me was helpful, what might it help you with?

C Well, everyone seems to think my problem is silly but to me it's not, it's really traumatic.

T So if this meeting helps you with that problem, would that make it useful to you?

C Well, yes, if it could.

Once the therapist and client have agreed an aim, it is possible to use the 'miracle question' to begin to define what the achievement of that aim might look like. Since the 'miracle' will be 'life without the problem', it will not even be necessary to know what the problem is. The therapist's ultimate knowledge about the problem will therefore be in the client's control. All the therapist has to do is follow, by taking seriously, everything that the client chooses to tell.

Therapist: So let's imagine that tonight, while you are asleep, a miracle happens and this problem is resolved, but you're asleep when it happens so you don't know about it. What's the first thing you'll notice tomorrow when you wake up that begins to tell you that this miracle has happened?

In this case, the client, referred by her doctor, was unsure whether or not brief therapy could help, so she came obliquely to the issue, not even sure that she wanted to say what the problem was. Not knowing the problem is not a hindrance to successful brief therapy, provided it is the client's choice. In this case the therapist was told later in the session that the miracle would be the absence of a very distressing visual hallucination. With help from a number of different professionals she was able to overcome this problem and get on with her life.

Another common situation is when the client is referred by an authority he or she cannot afford to ignore. Probation and child protection services are obvious examples. Despite the way clients of these services are often described, we find no less motivation than with other clients, provided we look in the right place, i.e. for what the client wants to achieve.

Therapist: So what are your hopes for this meeting?

Client: I haven't really got any.

T   So what decided you to come?

C   Well, I didn't have any choice. I was told I had to.

T   So how come you decided to go along with that?

C   They said if I didn't they'd take my kids away.

T   And you don't want that?

C   No, of course I don't!

T   So you decided that rather than risk losing your kids you'd come here?

C   Yes.

T   So if this meeting helps you hang on to your kids would that mean it had been worth your while coming?

C   Yes.

Once the client's goal, in this case to keep her children, is established it is possible for the Authority's goal, that is the protection of the children, to be included:

Therapist: So let's imagine that tonight, while you are asleep, a miracle happens, and your life starts moving in exactly the right direction for you so you keep your kids, so you are looking after your family in a way which is right for you and right for the authorities, what would you begin to notice different tomorrow which told you this miracle had happened?

In this 'miracle' the client's goal is fully honoured and so is the Authority's goal. The underlying assumption is that for all of us there are a variety of ways to 'do' our lives well. In the case of child abuse the Authority can legitimately impose limits on parental behaviour, for example, in relation to chastisement. It can also prescribe certain broad goals for parents to achieve, such as meeting the physical, emotional and educational needs of the child. But *how* the parent achieves these goals, provided they do so within the limits of acceptable child care practice, is the business of the parent. When the Authority steps into this business it will inevitably lead to conflict. In the miracle question quoted above the parent's goals and those of the Authority are included. Because the client is still free to choose their own way of parenting, co-operation and partnership are possible.

It is an arguable point whether or not all clients are motivated, but by *assuming* motivation it becomes our responsibility to *find* it (Iveson, 1996). If we don't find what we are looking for then we assume we have not asked the right questions and so are looking in the wrong place. Because there is no way of knowing for certain whether the client lacks motivation, or we simply have not found the right question to uncover it, we assume the failure is ours. The alternative is to begin to take a position in which we know better than our clients and from which we make judgments about them – an expert position which does not fit the underlying philosophy of the approach.

SMALL MIRACLES

The miracle question can be seen as a way of asking the client to invite us into his or her world, and our task is then to see *their* world, as it would be at its best, through *their* eyes. We have developed an approach to the question that seeks to define the smallest aspects of the client's life, sometimes right down to what they'd be having for breakfast! 'What will you notice that is different about your cornflakes?' is a question which might produce a smile, but it nearly always produces a potentially useful answer as well! The smaller the detail, the more do-able is the 'miracle' and the more attuned to the client's culture are the goals of the work.

It is this complete dependence of the therapist on the knowledge of the client which makes solution focused brief therapy so culturally mobile. With no culture-bound diagnostic framework, no way of 'knowing' the client from an outside observer's position, we have to accept the client's way of 'doing' their life, provided it is within the law, as the best way. This is just as true when the client is subject to statutory intervention. Even in these circumstances we do not have a view about what the client should do — only what they should not. The Authority is there only to prevent harm and it does not legitimately extend to saying how a client should live the day-to-day details of his or her life. Recognising this distinction and working out the client's way of living, within the law or within the limits set by the statutory authority, is one of the surest routes to co-operation and partnership in statutory work.

We have come to treat the client's answers to our detailed question as an invitation into their lives and homes and so find ourselves going with as much care and respect as we would expect from visitors to our own homes. The experience is often to feel very close to our clients without actually being a part of their lives: visitors but not participants.

FROM EXCEPTIONS TO TIMES WHEN THE MIRACLE IS ALREADY HAPPENING

When writing *Problem to Solution* we were just beginning to realise the significance of the 'miracle question', whereas now we would be hard pressed to do without it. Originally it had been a way to mark out the end-point of our work, and we used the identification and amplification of exceptions as the main route to change. As we realised the importance of clear and concrete goals, and so paid more attention to following up the 'miracle' we began to notice that the answers to the 'miracle' sequence seemed to have a therapeutic value in themselves. We also noticed that as the 'miracle' became more clearly defined, we and our clients started bumping into times when the miracle would already be happening. In the case of a woman with a very serious eating difficulty, the first sign of her 'miracle' occurred within the first few minutes of the session:

Therapist: So what would be the next sign of the miracle?

Client: I'd get up first.

T   Would your partner be surprised to see you get up first?

C   No, not straight away because some days I do get up before him anyway.

T   So that's a little bit of the miracle happening already?

C   Yes – sometimes.

'Times when the miracle already happens' is increasingly becoming an alternative to exploring exceptions and gives a more solution focused turn to the therapy since, unlike exception-finding, it has no direct connection to the problem. Our understanding of the therapeutic value of the 'miracle question', other than just as a definition of goals, is that putting into words the description of a 'do-able' future creates the possibility of it happening. A number of clients have commented on this process, none more movingly than another woman who had suffered serious eating difficulties for many years:

Client: For fifteen years I have been told and believed that this problem could never actually be cured, so each day I have had to make myself carry on. I've had to take every day as it comes and sometimes if it wasn't for my children I would have given up. But now I know that it is curable I'm going to try and get over it, I don't know if I'll be strong enough to but at least I'll have a go!

Therapist: What has made the difference? How come after only one session you can be so sure you can resolve things?

C You've taken me bit by bit through a whole day and with each of my answers I've been asking myself 'Can you do that, Catherine?' Each time I've been able to say 'Yes' so now I know that it's possible and I'm going to try!

In this session the therapist had spent thirty-five minutes following up the miracle question. Four sessions and four months later the woman was well on the way to reclaiming her life, and not only from the constraints of eating difficulties.

Examples of the 'miracle' already happening are usually abundant in sessions and give the therapist a number of choices: the 'miracle' exploration might be put on hold in order to explore and make more significant the fact that some part of it has already happened; or it may simply be registered for later use, for instance, as part of a scaling question: 'So would the fact that your partner sometimes does see you get up first be one of the factors that might make him think you are already at three on the scale?' Sometimes there are so many instances of the 'miracle' already happening that their own weight is enough to shift the balance without the therapist even pointing them out. In one case a teacher was describing her 'miracle' in respect of a child at risk of exclusion. It was only when she had described him coming in, sitting down quietly, answering the register, lining up and walking to assembly quietly that she realised these behaviours were already beginning to happen. So conscious was she of the difficulties the boy presented she had not noticed her own remarkable success in helping overcome them!

In solution focused therapy there are no quick fixes because no fixing is done. Anything that subsequently happens was already possible before the therapy, and whatever future the client moves into, its history was already present.

FROM SOLUTIONS TO 'A WAY OF LIVING'

As we have expanded our use of the miracle question we have found ourselves moving away from the idea of solutions. As de Shazer has said (de Shazer, 1988, 1991) the word 'solution' implies the word 'problem', since solutions are the result of problems being solved, and the less part the problem plays in our work the less room there is for solutions. At the same time we have learned to stay close to why the client has come –

which is usually to resolve a problem! When we ask our clients about their hopes for the session the most common response is to describe the problem they have come with. When the client has finished this description (which may be long or short), we will check if their hopes are to do with the resolution of that problem. If the answer is 'yes' then the miracle will be defined by the absence of that problem. (Occasionally the client is not coming in with hopes of a solution but merely for reassurance that they are handling a difficult situation well enough. In these circumstances, a miracle, which implies change, would not be addressing the client's goal. What would need to be explored instead is everything the client is doing which is working and what would tell them that it was still working tomorrow.) If the client's hopes are to be free from depression the miracle is defined, initially, by the absence of depression. But the subsequent answers do not uncover so much a solution as a way of living, in this case, without depression. What we sometimes refer to as a 'post-miracle quality of life'. Whatever problem a client presents with the miracle describes a way of living rather than any specific solution. It has been in our statutory work that some of these developments have been most marked. In the child protection case above, and in many others like it, the client is often struggling to maintain a sense of their own autonomy in the face of powerful authorities able to transform forever the client's way of living. Often, bids for autonomy are made in a way which produces even more unwanted attention: refusing to comply with 'contracts', shouting in case conferences and even breaking windows can be seen as attempts to show autonomy, but they rarely achieve a constructive end. In these fraught cases many of our questions will be around how the client does justice to themselves and their own beliefs in a way which gives them pride without harming their case. Once again the emphasis is on finding a way of living in which the client can feel satisfaction and pride: even in the face of external injustice.

Our experience has been that as we help clients do justice to themselves, get their lives back on track, live their lives in a way that suits them and suits those they love, they begin to find their own way forward. If moving forward means they have to resolve some specific problems in the process, then they are more likely to find their own resolutions than they are to use ours. This has been very apparent in our work with women who have been abused as children but do not want this to be the issue for therapy. As these women have moved forward in their lives they have often reported events, meetings or experiences which suggest that they are 'dealing with' their past experiences in a constructive way – having different conversations with family members, talking about the past with a 'safe' person, writing letters or just generally asserting themselves more.

BACK FROM THE FUTURE

Another application of this idea of 'doing justice to yourself' has been the rehearsal of a difficult event from the standpoint of its successful, but still future, completion. At times we all enter situations which we know can change our lives: a job interview is an obvious example. Our clients, with court appearances, case conferences, meetings with housing officers, psychiatrists, social workers and others in a position of power are, all too frequently, in situations where their performance for an hour can have a profound effect on their lives. Mrs. Ovinda was one such woman, with a case conference to attend and the real possibility of losing her children, especially if she was seen as continuing to be unco-operative. Her past behaviour at such conferences had been either to look at the floor and have no voice or to become very angry, verbally abusive and walk out. She thought neither of these behaviours would help her keep her children.

Therapist: Let's imagine the case conference is nearly over and you have been asked to wait outside while they have their final discussion. You're worried, of course, because you don't know what their decision is going to be, but you also know that you really did justice to yourself and to your children while you were in the meeting. You're feeling a sense of pride in yourself and think back to how you did it. What would you be remembering about how you were just before going into the conference?

Client: I would have been calm.

T   And what else?

C   I think I'd be nervous but I wouldn't want it to show.

T   What would you do instead?

C   I'd be thinking about what I was going to say.

T   And what else?

C   I'd be thinking it doesn't matter what they think about me – I know I love my kids!

T   And as you walk into the conference what sort of woman will they see?

C   I'd like them to see a strong woman.

T   So what would you be remembering that they'd seen which told them that this was a strong woman walking into the room?

C   Because I'd speak my mind.

T   And even before you spoke what would they have seen which told them that this was a strong woman?

C   They'd see it in my face.

T   What would they see?

C   I wouldn't be afraid to look at them – I'd have my head up.

T   Does that suit you, having your head up?

C   I don't know.

T   What do you think?

C   Yes it does!

Looking back from a successful, though hypothetical, future and tracing its apparent achievement has proved an extremely effective way to help clients do justice to themselves on those occasions when it most counts.

Another woman had rung in a state of near-suicidal desperation at the prospect of the housing department continuing to refuse to move her from the estate where she had been gang-raped – even though the rapists were at large and taunting her. A twenty-minute telephone conversation in which she described the impending meeting as if she had done justice to herself led to another call the following day. She was still awaiting a decision but wanted to reassure me that she was no longer feeling so desperate. She felt very proud of the way she had presented herself at the meeting with the housing officer and thought that even if she didn't get re-housed she could handle it. Later she explained why the process of the meeting had been more important than the actual outcome. The official view of the rape was that she was to blame, and because she blamed herself anyway she did not feel she had the power to argue. She also knew she had been seriously abused and blamed herself for not being stronger and standing up for herself. Lots of people had said she should stand up for herself and because she had not lived up to these expectations she felt even worse. The end product was that however badly she was treated it felt like it was really her own fault and that she had brought it on herself. After her meeting with the housing officer, when she felt she had stood up for herself in a way which made her feel proud, she knew that she would not take the blame for not being heard. If she didn't get a move it was because society was unfair, not because she was in some way unfit. This was an extremely moving story and brought home the final horror of so much abuse: that the abused person is somehow made to feel responsible. It is this sense of personal guilt which is often most corrosive in people's lives. We have no wish to help clients accept their 'lot in life', but we are interested helping them to do justice to themselves, even if the world remains unjust. As it was, the woman was re-housed.

SCALES, SCALES AND MORE SCALES

Our use of scales has grown with our clients' responses to them. We have also added zero to the scale since this more reflects where some clients feel they are. The zero-to-ten scale as a framework for encouraging clear and detailed descriptions has proved one of the most useful tools, and as long as the fulfillment of some aspect of the client's goal is represented by ten the scale framework remains totally relevant to the client's purpose in attending. Scales can be used to chart progress along any number of different aspects of a person's life: sobriety, financial security, relationship with child, parent or partner, safety, occupation, social life, mental health etc. Scales can also be used to obtain the client's ideas about how significantly others perceive the situation: 'Where do you think your wife/social worker/the case conference chairperson/the magistrate/the head teacher would put you on this scale?' begins to provide the client with clues about the way forward in respect of significant others. It does not always have to be totally serious!

Therapist: So if Mary could count (and speak!) where do you think she would place you on the scale?

Client: Oh, Mary knows exactly what's going on!

T   So where would she put you?

C   About 3.

T   About 3. What would she be seeing that makes her go that high?

C   Well, I do take her out sometimes.

T   How come?

C   Well someone has to!

T   Yes, but how come that when things are so desperate for you, you still think about Mary and not only think about her but follow it through with action?

C   I can't just ignore her!

T   Yes you could.

C   But I wouldn't. I couldn't do that!

T   Yet there must be times when it takes just sheer courage to walk out of the door.

C   But I don't always have that courage.

T   And sometimes you do?

C   Yes.

T   So what would Mary be noticing that told her things had moved
    from 3 to 4?

An apparently frivolous question can be both light-hearted and very
serious, and pets can provide a great opportunity for lightening an
interview without deflecting from its purpose. In this case a man who
had been 'unable' to leave his flat for two years still took his dog for a
walk. As is common with 'exceptions' the man saw this as evidence of his
problem since he could only go for walks at 4 o'clock in the morning.
Helping him, with the use of scales, to see that going out at all was a step
in the right direction helped him towards expanding his possibilities and
the eventual resolution of his 'agoraphobia'.

   Scales also lend themselves to visual representation and can be
extremely useful when there is no common language or in other
situations where words are difficult to come by. Jenny Grinstead of Save
the Children Fund, which has a project in Ipswich treating families in
which there has been sexual abuse, has adapted solution focused brief
therapy to this particularly difficult area of work. In a family session with
Donna, a four-year-old who had been abused by her brother and who
had refused to speak to any professional for many weeks, Jenny had been
asking the older members of the family to scale their assessment of
Donna's safety. Meanwhile, Donna, playing to one side with a box of
toys, had been placing farm animals in rows of ten! Taking her cue Jenny
asked: 'If this sheep means you are frightened and worried all the time
and this elephant (on a farm!) means you are not worried or frightened
at all, which animal would you be at today?' Donna thought for about
five seconds and chose a duck, number six in the line. Jenny asked her
what made her know she was that much safe, and Donna dug into the
toy box and brought out mother and daughter dolls. Donna agreed with
Jenny's understanding that her mother being with her more was one of
the contributors to her safety. When Jenny asked what would be different
when her safety and lack of worry reached the pig (number 7) Donna
once again dug into the box and produced father and son dolls putting
them close together. 'So if your daddy does more with your brother will
that make things better for you?' Nod. 'So what do you think they'd be
doing together?' 'Going to football,' said Donna, speaking for the first
time!

SCALES AND MULTIPLE PROBLEMS

Scales also allow the therapist to address several problems in one session.
One woman came into therapy weighed down by life and its

disappointments. She lived in a flat which she hated, did a job she despised, was in a relationship with a married man, had no friends, was unloved by her family and in constant arguments with her mother. She was 46 and her hopes of living a 'normal life with a husband and children' were to remain unfulfilled.

The session took the shape of a 'broad brush stroke' miracle in which her new hopes were merely sketched out: a different flat, a more satisfying job, a social life, a committed relationship, getting on with her mother and family and taking up photography again. The rest of the session was taken up with scales. The first was an overall scale with 0 being that she had 'given up' (feeling like giving up had been one of her reasons for seeking help) and 10 being the full-blown miracle. She was at 2 with a realistic target of 7. After a brief exploration of this scale, each of the specific issues was scaled: home, job, relationship, family, mother, social life and photography. All the scales were under 2 and for each at least one specific concrete detail was sought on what she was doing to 'keep it off the bottom'. Similar detail was then obtained about how she would recognise a rise of half a point (when the client is very low on a scale, half points often work better than whole ones – they are more in keeping with the client's mood). With this number of scales not long can be spent on each one but as long as each provides its share of detail, together they build a very strong picture of possibility. The client is also left with a sense that every issue has been addressed. The final technique with multiple scales is to knit them together. At the beginning of the session the client will often feel all their problems are glued together in one inextricable mass. This is why trying to prioritise so often proves frustrating. The scales provide a way of unraveling the tangle so each problem is isolated and each comes with a resource and a possible improvement. If towards the end of the session the therapist invites the client to consider what might happen to one scale as a result of an improvement on another, the problems become reconnected but in a constructive way:

Therapist: If you were to go up half a point on your job scale what effect do you think it might have on your relationship with your mother scale?

Client (*After some thought*): It would have an effect. Sometimes I'm so strung up with this job I'm sure I take it out on my mother.

T   And if you went up half a point on your photography scale what effect do you think that might have on your housing scale?

C (*More thought*) Half my problem is that I feel so depressed I don't get on and do things. If I was actually getting on with *something* I think I'd feel better and maybe do the place up a bit.

T   And if you were socialising just a little bit more what effect might that have on your job scale?

C   I'd feel more confident for a start, so I might start believing I could do something different.

Which scales are linked together does not seem to matter, mostly the client finds a positive connection.

Client: On the way here I felt my life was complicated.

Therapist: Well, I have to say that I entirely agree!

C   Yes, but it doesn't feel that way now – it feels like I can go and do anything and whatever it is it will help things along.

T   So have you anything in mind?

C   Yes, I'm going to get my camera out *(pause)*. Isn't that weird! Last night I was doing a bit of clearing up and I came across my camera, so I got it out – I'd completely forgotten until now

T   It sounds like you might be on your way already!

CUTTING THE CLOTH

How a session goes in terms of the balance of time spent on exploring miracles, uncovering exceptions and constructing scales, is partly influenced by the client and partly by a relatively arbitrary choice by the therapist. If the morning has been spent in the microcosmic world of 'cornflake miracles' the therapist might choose to lead an afternoon client into a more scale-based session, like the one just described. If the client mentions an exception which the therapist believes to be especially significant, the therapist might follow this line even if the exception was mentioned during responses to the miracle question. Every session offers almost countless opportunities for curiosity about the client's preferred future and what is already being done to get there.

The variety of opportunities created by solution focused brief therapy thinking makes it adaptable to very different situations.

The twenty second session

Therapist *(At the ticket office, King's Cross Railway Station, London, handing over the 'Brief Therapy Practice' payment card):* A return to Newcastle coming back Friday, please.

Ticket seller *(Looking at the card):* Mm brief therapy – I could do with some of that!

T   So how would you know if it had worked?

Ts *(Laughing)* Oh, I'd know alright!

T   How would you know?

Ts *(Thoughtfully)* That's a good question. Sign here please, sir.

The twenty second session

Josie and Desmond were referred because of marital violence, alcoholism and child protection issues. Most of the work was done in the first five sessions, but there was an expectation that they continue to attend therapy. As there was also a court hearing pending the couple did not want to prejudice their case. Most of the subsequent sessions were aimed at helping Josie and Desmond cope with the 'goldfish bowl' life they were leading. One of the great dilemmas in child protection work is how to balance the necessity of monitoring against the adverse effects it has on a family's ability to cope. The sessions with Desmond and Josie were routinely based around two questions: what have you done since we last met which has helped keep you on track, and what will you see yourselves doing next week which tells you you are still on track? Over the year that the work took place there were many ups and downs. Paying attention to what the client is doing which is helpful is not to ignore setbacks. It is when the client suffers setbacks that what they do which is helpful becomes especially important. At one meeting the couple had had their child removed a few days previously because of an episode of their drinking. They were distraught, had argued but there had been no violence. Neither had they drunk again since the incident. Exploring how they had managed not to turn to drink and how, with such a terrible argument Josie had remained safe, was part of their route forward, but until it was put into words they had been feeling as though they were going backwards. The twenty-second session was the one before their final court appearance. Reviewing everything they had achieved was helpful towards feeling personal confidence the next day. Asking them to describe how this inner confidence would show in court gave them a chance to rehearse being at their best. The couple were reported to have done great justice to themselves the next day in court and they left feeling that justice was also done *to* them. They had their child returned.

The same ideas can be used in an eight-minute appointment by a general practitioner: 'I can see things are not going well for you. What have been your ways of coping with depression during the past week?'... 'If these new tablets were to do the trick what would be the first sign that they were helping?'

THE INVISIBLE THERAPIST

Clients sometimes give feedback of their own at the end of a session. These two examples were particularly informative!

> 'When you are asking the right questions you disappear – its only when you are asking irrelevant ones that I notice you!'

This is an excellent illustration of how it is the client who is doing the work, but it is no wonder some people think we haven't been much help to them – even when the problem is resolved!

During a third and last session, while reviewing the amazing progress a woman had made overcoming the effects of abuse and drug use, she said:

> 'I hope you won't be offended by this but I do feel I've got to say it. I know coming here has probably saved my life but I want you to know that you still haven't played any part in that. Though you are important in one way you are not part of my life.'

It was, in fact, as good a compliment as a brief therapist could hope to receive. Insoo Kim Berg (in an Internet discussion) put it most succinctly: 'Good brief therapists leave no footprints in their clients' lives!'

CHAPTER THREE

SMOKE GETS IN YOUR EYES: A case of depression

'I think it is particularly helpful to think of problems as stories that people have agreed to tell themselves,' (Hoffman, 1990). 'Families are wonderful story-tellers because they have such interesting scripts to describe. They come to therapy with these scripts tightly written... As clinicians we offer the family new scripts...' (Cecchin, 1987).

Joyce and David Dawes, a white couple, certainly came to therapy with a tightly-written script and with a problem story to which both of them fully subscribed. David's previous experience of therapy in his first marriage had probably helped with the fine-tuning of the couple's story, such that therapy seemed the only appropriate course of action. It was David who made the referral, contacting the clinic to say that Joyce was depressed and had been for a year and a half. He was asking for help on her behalf and he was more than happy to attend with her.

Joyce, coming up to fifty, was in her third marriage at the time of referral. She was in close contact with two adult children from her first marriage. Both her parents lived in the North of England. Since coming to London Joyce had worked as a nursery assistant. David was older than Joyce and had retired early from a business career which had been hampered by depression. He also had two children from his first marriage. Joyce and David had been together for approximately four years.

Joyce's attunement to the couple's idea of therapy and what would be involved led her, in the first half-hour of the first session, to tell the therapist that she had been sexually abused as a child, and that her relationship with her parents had never been resolved and remained problematic. Joyce stated that her mother had blamed her while her father had never apologised and had never accepted responsibility. She also told the therapist that she had been abused in her two previous marriages, that she had begun to entertain serious doubts about how good her parenting of her own children had been, that she was depressed and had suffered a loss of 'personhood'. She was well able, in the first session, to describe her current state in detail, namely copious and repeated weeping, a loss of confidence and of any sense of excitement, such that she was not working, not going out and not taking care of herself.

Solution focused therapists develop with their clients new and more complex stories. The beginning point of this new complexity is often the idea that alongside the problem pattern the client already has in place, one, or many, solution patterns that are already effective in diminishing, limiting and restricting the problem. An exploration which provokes the discovery of the co-existence of problem and solution patterns can be the basis of the first loosening in the story that the client agrees to tell him or herself. As this changes, so does the client's way of being. The therapist, within this approach, learns to develop a sensitive 'constructive ear' (Lipchik, 1988) which picks up from the client's conversation and actively shapes the conversation in such a way as to elicit different elements already occurring in the client's life. This 'new information' can then make more visible to the client his or her solution patterns. This procedure contrasts strongly with most clients' expectations of the process of therapy, in that it minimises the opportunities for an increase in guilt, blame and sense of failure. Indeed the therapist actively attempts to direct the conversation in such a way as to reduce feelings of guilt, blame and failure, all of which, it can be argued, inhibit personal creativity and imaginativeness which are important ingredients in the development of the solution pattern.

The work with the Dawes family illustrates just such a change of script.

FIRST SESSION

Therapist: I know very little of what's brought you here today.

Joyce: It's basically for me. That's the main thing. For about a year and a half I've been suffering from depression. I've had many things happen to me in my life. I've been the kind of person who when things happened I'd be inclined to get nervous about them but I'd still cope.

T   What kind of things?

Joyce goes on to describe normal life cycle issues, compounded by the experience of having been on her own for a considerable time bringing up her children. The discussion provides opportunities for the therapist to highlight the 'coping', thus already bringing Joyce's coping strengths into the therapy in a way that may serve to minimise a subsequent sense of failure and worthlessness. Only five minutes have elapsed, the problem is by no means clear, indeed has only been mentioned in passing, but the therapist is already beginning to cue into solutions. Joyce introduces the idea of her 'coping' past to contrast with the present.

J   ...things that happened. Some of them quite drastic in their way but

I always managed to cope Well, I mean, I managed in my own way.

T   Sure.

J   I might get nervous, things like that, but I never really got depressed except in the way that people say, 'I'm feeling a bit depressed, under the weather', but not this, what I've got now, this lethargy I've also got. To pick up a telephone to speak to people, to go out to the shop was a great difficulty, or not *was* but *is* sometimes.

T   'Is' at the moment or…

J   Well actually I'm getting a little bit better. I can feel there's something happening. I'm not as bad as I was.

Moments such as these are the nodal points of therapy, moments when there is an obvious choice: two (at least) directions which will lead to quite different narratives. The therapist still knows virtually nothing about the problem but is being offered a potential approach to solution. For the solution focused therapist the choice is clear, particularly since the solution track, at this moment, leads towards a conversation about how change was brought about before the beginning of therapy, before any possibility of therapy stealing any of the credit (Weiner-Davis et al, 1987). The client can always be 'blamed' (Kral and Kowalski, 1989) with confidence for improvement before therapy has started.

T   Since when? Since when has that change happened?

J   Well, actually it started about November would you say *(to David)* until I got that set-back.

D   October.

T   *(counting on fingers)* October, November, December…

D   December there was a bit of a drama.

The couple start to describe the 'set-back'. Another moment of choice.

T   Do you think you've moved back now, to where you were before the set-back?

The therapist does not know what the 'set-back' is.

J   Not quite now but I'm starting… there's things I'm being able to do now that I couldn't do…

T   Great. What sort of things?

J   I've sometimes got to push myself really, really hard…

T   Yes.

J   Sometimes.

T   Are you someone who can do that? Who's quite tough with yourself?

J   Well, everyone used to be of the opinion Joyce is super, she has confidence, Joyce is a goer, she doesn't let anything get her down.

Now basically this was a big front with me. I had to because of my children. I wasn't as confident as I appeared to be. But I had to be.

T   But you had to be.

J   It was necessary and I was…

T   You did it.

J   So therefore I've got a determination if it's necessary you see but I think maybe then I was needed. My children needed me.

T   So at that point that was something you could draw on.

During this brief interchange Joyce accepts the idea that her toughness is not just a front but is a part of herself. She has volunteered the idea that she can produce 'confidence' when 'it was necessary' and has stated that she has 'determination'. Even though Joyce has contextualised these successes ('My children needed me') the therapist is aware that the task of producing familiar behaviour in a new environment is far more manageable than facilitating the generation of totally new behaviours.

J   I think because I had to cope for my children's sake I did, but now I'm facing me and some of the things I'm seeing I don't like, and there are other things I'm finding out that I do like, starting to…

T   Give me, just so I can begin to get a picture of where things are at the moment… you said you're beginning to be able to do some things that in the past you'd find difficult. What sort of things are you beginning to do?

J   Like being able to take calls, telephone calls.

T   OK. So you can answer the phone now, pick up the phone, deal with it…

J   There are some days still, like the other day I couldn't do it…

T   But by and large.

J   By and large that's a lot better. The thought of getting myself up to go to the shops was a great difficulty. I mean…

T   And now?

J   That's not so bad now, that's also getting better.

T   Good. What have you done that's helped you to… what's the difference that's made a difference?

The interchange at this point in the session is ideal for a solution focused therapist. The therapist is finding out about the problem in the context of the client's successes in relation to the problem. This can lead very simply to a question regarding the client's solution pattern, 'What have you done that's helped you to… what's the difference that's made a difference?' The shift of emphasis from problem-talk to solution-talk can include the search for exceptions, or an examination of recent progress, or the route taken in the following segment approximately one minute after the last interchange:

J I lost all confidence in myself in almost every aspect. I've got a reasonably good wardrobe and I've even still, yes, a basic three items, three things that I wear...

T So that's something that you'd like to see more movement in...

J Yes. I'm not taking the same interest. I'm keeping to three outfits. I've got quite a few holes.

T That would be a way that you would know that things were moving on a bit more, when you begin to have more variety.

The problem that is raised in this segment is therefore immediately woven into a goal for change and indeed into a marker that will indicate that change is happening. At points in therapy when there is a danger that the client will be overwhelmed by feelings of defeat emanating from the past, a shift to a future focus can empower the client, leading to an expectation of greater control in his or her life. Joyce, however, returns to the theme of her past difficulties, although beginning increasingly to pepper her conversation with lead-ins to exceptions and change. This return to problem-talk evokes from the therapist a blunter move. He changes the subject politely:

T (to David) Can I just ask Mr. Dawes for a moment... you said that the change started in October?

D Yes.

T What was it that you began to see in October? Just again to give me an idea... sometimes someone observing...

D (to Joyce) You were complaining less of headaches. I mean, for a long time Joyce would wake with a severe headache, and that was passing. General enthusiasm. There was a sort of look of anxiety that was going. There was a worry line here (indicates forehead) when she was, that was for me an indicator of Joyce's mood.

T Yes.

D That worry line was not so prevalent and generally speaking she was more sociable. First of all you (to Joyce) had less physical symptoms, less backaches, less headaches and less of various aches and pains and things and your mood was generally better. Those were the most obvious things. And also we were talking about the future. Whereas before...

T The two of you started talking again about future plans?

D Yes, whereas for a long time everything we shelved...

T   ,,,day-to-day…
D   It was very much day-to-day…
T   Is that something that is continuing Mr. Dawes?
D   Recently more so, with a certain trepidation because some of our
     plans are fairly dramatic. We're planning to move to Spain…
T   It's not chicken-feed.
D   No, no, it's a big, complete change in our whole lives. That's really
     the main thing…
T   That's what you see. Do you have any explanation? I always…
J   How it came about?
T   Yes, how things began to take an up-turn?

At this point Joyce answers a different question that she thought she
heard, how things had taken a down-turn. This produces three extremely
difficult life-events and leads her to link back to her own experience of
being sexually abused as a child:

J   As a young teenager I suffered severe abuse from my father.
D   Twelve, thirteen years old.
J   And… *(pause)*
T   Was that something you'd talked about?
J   Not really. Very, very seldom did I talk about it. My mother
     occasionally, she brought it up but not in the way it should have
     been.
D   Not in a constructive way.
T   So you brought it up at the time.

Joyce talks more about the abuse, moving on to the more general issue
of her parenting and her doubts about it. The therapist acknowledges
the experience of abuse and other difficult recent events and goes on to
ask:

T   How do you explain that in October last year your mood began to
     lighten and you began to…?
J   I don't really know.
D   We talked a lot about it.
T   You two.
J   David's been marvellous with me, the patience he's had…
T   Do you find that that helps when the two of you talk?
J   Sometimes. Sometimes I don't want him to.
D   Sometimes it's painful and then I have to back off…
T   Right.
D   And leave it.

J   There's times I just have to be on my own and I just   it's not fair but he deals with it... but we are able at times... I'm starting to remember things that I'd forgotten all about and I find that I've got a terrible rage inside me.

D   I was aware of this.

T   Yes

D   Rage inside her.

T   Are they things that go way way back, connected with the abuse?

J   Yes. Yes. I thought I'd handled it and I thought that I'd closed that part off and it didn't hurt me and it was alright really... but it hasn't been alright and I feel this, really anger and hurt and it's like I was saying to you (to David).

T   I guess people take things on when they're ready to... somehow you were ready to take it on now.

J   Yes. I don't cry so much now. I used to have terrible, terrible fits of crying, just burst into tears.

Joyce goes on giving more detail, which continues to differentiate past acute distress and her present state.

T   Would you say that this time you've been able to experience the feelings much more powerfully than at any time in the past?

J   Yes.

T   Yes.

J   Yes.

T   ...and there are more memories about what happened?

J   Yes.

T   Who... you talk with Mr. Dawes about this?

J   Yes.

T   Do you have other people you talk to about it or is it being kept mainly within...?

J   There have been one or two that I've skated the surface with but I never went into it with any detail.

T   Yes you have to judge, don't you.

J   David knows more about it than anyone else. Even any of my family. My children, they know that there was something happened.

T   So there's been a very very significant issue for you that you've been struggling with this year.

Although these extracts illustrate only a limited range of directions available to the solution oriented therapist in talking about sexual abuse, it should be clear that Joyce easily accepts the idea that she may now be ready to deal with the past, highlighting of course her growth and her readiness to accept as growth her more powerful feelings and her new memories . In addition the conversation has established at least two things that are useful to Mrs. Dawes in moving on, sometimes talking to her husband and sometimes not talking. The therapist might have chosen to establish a goal in relation to dealing with the experience of abuse, using perhaps the 'miracle question', and then to have discussed with Joyce and David what, in their views the first small sign of change may be. In this particular case the sense of change and momentum already percolating throughout the session is in evidence here as well, and further work in relation to the abuse at this stage seemed unnecessary to the therapist.

Joyce develops the theme of childhood abuse in relation to her current interaction with her mother. Her experience of being unable to challenge mother and feeling obliged to always accommodate to her brings her down, even though a number of exceptions and recent innovations are noted on the way. In order to re-evoke the sense of change the therapist introduced a scaling task, asking Joyce to imagine a scale on which 10 represents the worst things have ever been for her and 0 represents the way she would want things to be following a miracle, and to place herself on the scale. Joyce's response that last year she had been at 10, but now she oscillated between 7/8 on bad days and 4/5 on good days facilitated a discussion which re-established what it was that good days looked like. The therapist's questions served to establish a matrix of optimistic behaviours that suggested a prescription for improvement and re-established a future focus, a way forward.

Returning to Mr. and Mrs. Dawes after the consulting break, the therapist was able to acknowledge both the life difficulties experienced by Mrs. Dawes and the marked positivity in the way the couple were moving and, in addition, many changes that had taken place in Mrs. Dawes' own behaviour, in the couple's interactions, in Mrs. Dawes' relations with her mother and with her children.

T   On top of all that, what I'm struck by is how you've been able to talk much more openly with Mr. Dawes about your abuse, your sexual abuse in childhood, and what I heard you say is that you told Mr. Dawes more than you'd ever told anyone about what happened and I'm sure that you both know that the talking and the naming what happened is not the first step in dealing with it, but it's the second or third step in moving towards actively dealing with it...

D   Resolving it...

T That's right, and I guess what you'll notice is that as you do more of that, more of the sharing, more of the talking with Mr. Dawes you might find that you begin to talk to others in a less guarded way and I guess that you'll notice that as a sign that you're moving on. So, a lot of difficulties in the year but a staggering number of changes as well, latterly, and really very important ones in relation to mother, in relation to children and in relation to your past, you know, of the sexual abuse.

J Yes. You see I fall back again into the old traps, although I make that start...

T Sure, no one would ever say that progress is a smooth line. Most progress is two steps forward and one back and two forward and one back and maybe two back then three forward, that's the way that progress happens. For anyone to imagine that progress happens in a nice smooth line...

J It's not like that.

T It's not like that and in fact our view is that the two forward and one back progress is more stable than the straight line. It needs to be tested against reality. You know, tested against weight of reality. What I'd like you to do is something rather trivial – this is the first time we've met. We've begun to, you know, get to know a little bit of what's going on. I'd just like you to do something for me, to notice the days that are 4 days and notice what's different about the 4 days from the 7 to 8 days, just to pay particular attention and to focus down on the 4 days and notice what's good about them, notice what you do on those days that's good for you.

SECOND SESSION

Mr. and Mrs. Dawes arrived late for this session which took place one week later. They had been out for a meal the night before and Mrs. Dawes was suffering from food poisoning:

T What have you been doing that's been good for you in the last week apart from going out?

J I've had really a couple of very good days.

T Have you?

J Yes, I've also had some very very bad as well – it went from one extreme to the other, and then I've had a happy medium in between.

T How many of the very good days were there?

J I think maybe two.

T   Right, put of seven out of the week some of the others in between...
J   ...were not bad days but there were three out of those seven days - not all of the day -
T   Not all of the day.
J   But for a part of it that I was sweating profusely...

The therapist re-introduces the scale from the previous week and establishes amid a welter of changes, differences and exceptions that the best days were rated by Joyce at '2/3', the first time that she had reached this level for a very considerable time. Examining what it was that happened differently on these exceptionally successful days, Joyce noted that David and she had been talking even more than usual:

J   Things that I was afraid perhaps he would judge me on, because I'm always scared... it's always happened to me in my life – I don't think he does – I've told him a little bit now. 'Can I go a little bit further and tell him this?' and I think how nice can someone be and not judge you. So we've actually spoken, what happened with my ex-husband, the last straw that broke the camel's back if you like.
T   This was the new area that you began to discuss with David was it?
J   Yes, because what happened then made me feel very much less a woman. I felt betrayed, dirty, everything that went with it and I was able to tell him, the first person that I was ever...
T   Really? Great! So you were able to take more risks in your relationship with David. What was it that made it possible for you to do that?

Joyce has understood the compliment from the last session as a task, and Joyce and David have moved rapidly into new areas of sharing, which in the previous session Joyce had stated was useful for her. Specifying what David did that helped her to talk, Joyce goes on to suggest that the talking was 'very emotional... like shedding a skin.'

Moving to David to elicit his recollections of Joyce's good days produces something different. He had noted that Joyce had started some days badly but had been able 'To get [herself] going, to get into gear.' Examining in detail these exceptions which held the possibility of converting 'bad day' to 'good day' led to the idea that Joyce could do this:

T   Have there been other days when you've been able to do that, when you've started down and been able to get yourself up?
J   Yes.
D   Apart from that you also booked your holiday, you went to the

dentist.

J   Yes, I've been to the dentist. I've been putting the dentist off. I hate the dentist but I have been doing things that I'm really – it's not like I'm doing it with joy, I'm pushing – I'm making myself do it.

T   How are you doing that because that sounds new or relatively new?

J   Yes it is a bit because I was so lethargic.

Joyce also begins to recognise that by and large when she can 'get herself into gear' it is 'for others'. One of these 'others' can be David, and Joyce indicates that sometimes she protests that he is not her 'doctor', not her 'keeper', 'leave me alone'.

This theme is picked up in the last segment of the session:

T   *(to David)* Was it round about that time that you were increasingly invited to take over?

D   Yes. Because I saw the effort, the dread for Joyce of going into the office, that I started driving her in rather than her taking the bus...

T   You made things easier for her.

J   Yes, he did.

T   How's it going to be for you, as what I'm hearing is that Joyce is beginning to take back some of the areas that were her areas before and that you, David, were invited into because there was a vacuum. How's it going to be for you giving those areas up again?

D   Delighted. Not just... it's not such an effort. We'd be back to where we were before this whole depression started.

T   And that was a more equal share of responsibility?

D   Yes, I would give a hand. I've never...

J   Incidentally, he's a very good cook himself.

T   *(to Joyce)* Maybe this is going to go too far and it'll be back in your court...

J   I'm very thankful to David and I appreciate it but there is, I've never said this, but it's true that it's like I'm always being watched every mood, swing, change, everything that I do, 'why did you do that?' He doesn't do that but sometimes I go overboard and I feel that.

T   Do you think that in the course of the last year when things haven't been easy that maybe David's become even more, you know, triply and quadruply sensitive to changes in mood and that as things continue to improve there'll be a few more rough edges that you'll bounce up against each other a bit more and that'll be OK? Because I've noticed *(to David)* that you're very attentive, aren't you? I don't know if you're that sort of person who is very attentive and always has been very attentive or whether that's been the product of a year in which you've had to cosset Joyce and surround her in cotton-wool.

D   Yes. That I've done consciously. I've made the effort to be aware of what's happening with Joyce... I've trained myself to notice things...

T   To notice.

D   Yes.

T   I've noticed that, lighting cigarettes and passing them to her and helping (*Joyce*) take her coat off at the beginning and it's as if you've become quadruply sensitive and maybe Joyce is saying she can cope with some rougher edges.

After the consulting break the therapist is able to return with a range of compliments: the fact of Joyce's determination to take on her depression and her exploration of ways of motivating herself; her decision that she no longer needs to be cosseted; the way both Joyce and David are taking risks, Joyce sharing more and David inviting more sharing in a way that could lead to rejection; and finally the flexibility of Joyce and David's relationship, the ebb and flow of their mutuality as David moves in to help out but is then able to back off. The team notes that as David gives ground, as he becomes aware that he will not need to be so sensitive all the time, so he might not need to surround Joyce in cotton-wool. Finally:

T   In the past you talked about how you geared yourself up when someone else or someone important is involved, you know when David was down in the summer you made yourself do what you believed was necessary to support David through that time. And again, I'm sure there are lots more examples if you look for them...

D   Yes.

T   Another very small example from last Friday. Your friend asked you for something [help] in relation to Charles and you responded because a friend was asking.

D   You do that a lot darling.

T   At the beginning of the session Joyce said that today she'd driven herself to get here because she thought it would be good for her. And that was something that I was hearing different. That it would be good for you, not for David, not for Charles' Mum, not for someone else, not for your Mum but good for you and we noticed that and began to get excited about that. OK that it was you driving yourself to do something that was good for you. What we'd like you to do between now and the next time we meet is just to begin to notice the times when you get yourself going just for you – not for David, not for your Mum, not for your children, not for anybody

else, just for you, and to notice how that seems to you, what the
spin-off is, what the pay-off is for you, what you get out of it...

J   I've never looked at it like that...

T   Because our guess is that there's a large field for you to explore and
enjoy and our guess is that you're going to do more of it.

THIRD SESSION

Mr. and Mrs. Dawes return to the Clinic three weeks later. In the
meantime, Mrs. Dawes had taken a planned two-week holiday with her
mother in Portugal, and Mr. Dawes had joined them for just a few days.
The holiday has been an exceedingly difficult experience for Mrs.
Dawes, who had not been in such close proximity to her mother for
many years. Despite the difficulties, Mrs. Dawes' narrative is full of
differences, of changes, of standing up to her mother, of holding her
own, of not backing away from confrontation. The therapist builds up a
sense of the extremity of the position Mrs. Dawes put herself in with her
mother in Portugal, this a previously anxious woman who had felt unable
to answer the phone:

T   How long were you there with your mother on your own?

D   Just over a week.

J   Just over a week.

T   Just over a week. So during that time you were effectively in charge
of things, in charge of managing things.

D   Yes.

T   Yes.

J   Yes, she wasn't well. I mean she really wasn't well during the first
week so nothing really untoward happened...

T   That was quite a test you put yourself in.

J   It was, actually. Because I was really worried at one point, I was
thinking I'd have to come back, because she... she really wasn't well
at all then.

T   How do you rate how you stood up to that test that you put yourself
in, being in a foreign context with a mother who wasn't well with
potential explosions and sickness balanced against that and being in
charge of things?

J   Well, I mean really it's the old story, you find resources inside
yourself that you didn't know you had. I was dreading doing this
because I was thinking, 'What if this happens, what if that happens,
how am I going to cope?' But I coped...

T   Yes.

J   I did alright, although I was scared.

T   That's different. So you found some resources in yourself.

J   I thought well, like there's weeks, months that I've thought I'm a pretty useless person, I can't do this, I can't do that, I can't even go out for a paper and there I was coping with my mother and I thought...

T   Yes. I'm struck by the difference.

J   I did it. I'm not too bad.

T   What else does this tell you about yourself? Because, I mean, those two weeks must have told you quite a lot about yourself.

J   Well, I think it's told me that, really, I'm coming out of my depression...

T   It sounds like you're regaining.

J   I'm regaining, but I hope that I'm more than regaining.

T   That you've moved on beyond it.

J   This is what I'm hoping, that I've moved beyond it. I don't want the old slot that I'm going to run and cope just because they need me. It's because what *I* want, *I* need... me was forgotten about a lot of times.

The recuperative holiday for Joyce's mother and the conversation in therapy about it has offered the opportunity, first to re-describe and to re-create Joyce's strength in coping 'for others' and, in addition, to explore the times that Joyce did what she wanted, did something different in relation to mother and did not feel guilty. She had also created a new goal – not just 'recovery' but advancement: she was going to become a person who did things not only for other people but also for *herself*. Building from here the therapist introduces a future projection, not a future hope or fantasy, but a projection of where Joyce sees herself in a year's time:

T   Where's all this going to take you? What image do you have, if you think on a year? Where's the development of that difference because you're talking about a difference not just going back to where you were a year ago but being someone who's got those skills and those qualities and those talents but who can also do things a bit differently now? Where do you see that taking you in a year's time?

J   Yes.

T   Is it quite misty at the moment or is...?

J   Yes it is. I think I know what's going to happen with *(to David)* our future together but as myself I hope that I'm going to become a stronger person. I think that I may, through this depression, I may

have learned something… And I also think I'm coming out, I can
see the light at the end of the tunnel and it's not a train with its
head-light blazing now, it's a slower train and I'm going to manage
to jump out of the way but save some of myself in the process which
has been lost for a long, long time not just at the time of the
depression but long before that.

T   That sounds very exciting.

J   Yes. I'm finding little parts of me that I wasn't aware of before.

T   You're re-discovering them.

J   Yes.

T   Bits that are quite new or bits that you were quite familiar with in the
past?

J   No, that are new actually.

T   New bits.

J   Quite new.

T   OK. So a year ahead it's quite misty how it's going to be. Have you
got any picture of how it'll be as you develop, hold this respect for
yourself really and respect for your own needs, have you got any
images of where that might take you?

J   Well, I don't. I don't have any image of that but what I want, what I
think, I'll become a nicer person perhaps, nicer to myself, to like
myself better.

T   OK. So what's that going to do when you do that? How's that going
to be when you build on that, liking yourself more?

J   I haven't got a picture but just common-sense thinking about it. I'm
going to have, I think, if you like yourself other people are going to
like you for what you are. I think before I was more of a selfless
person and I think out of this I might become more of a deeper
person.

T   OK.

J   Like when I wanted to tell someone off, they were hurting me, I
would hide it instead of telling them what I thought – or if, whatever
it was, always my feelings were hidden. I was like a shield, I hid
behind a shield and now I might – I think this is what might happen
without having fear of an argument – that I'd be able to say to
someone, 'No, I don't like that, what you're doing,' not to have an
argument about it.

T   To take a position?

J   To take a position, to make a stand for myself. I know that I don't
have to be always nice and a goody-goody little girl for people to like

me.

T   Do you have any inkling about how David's going to see this change developing?

The therapist pursues the impact on David of these part-projected, part-already achieved changes, asking Joyce whether she thinks David will cope and asking him the same question. Both reassure the therapist and Joyce returns to her previous theme, re-stating that she doesn't care if people like her, she now knows she's not bad or horrible and knows that she has merits. The future projection, although vague, has served a purpose, emphasising the continuity between behaviours already being achieved in the present and the hopes and expectations for the future.

Following the consulting break, the therapist acknowledges the impossibility of feeding back to Mr. and Mrs. Dawes all the positive things that the team had noticed, since this would take just as long as the session! The change was summarised for the couple in one, symbolic observation:

T   Just picking out one thing that was very visible to us as a change, was that today you lit your own cigarette. In the past it was almost as if David would have to light it for you and hand it to you, but today you controlled it and lit your own. Very striking about how you're incorporating change into your relationship. Great. We're very impressed and we certainly have a sense that everything you're doing, *everything you're doing,* is on the right track.
    (Joyce laughs).

On the basis of this session Mr. and Mrs. Dawes were offered a choice, either the opportunity to return in six weeks time to let us know what else they had done, or to finish work at this point. The couple elected to finish.

DISCUSSION

de Shazer assumes that theoretically it is possible to work successfully with a client without ever knowing the specific nature of the problem because there is a discontinuity between the problem pattern and the solution pattern. Mr. and Mrs. Dawes went some way towards demonstrating the reality of this possibility. The problems this couple was encountering were defined almost entirely by the exceptions and the changes. The therapist's 'constructive ear' meant that the nature of the problem was relatively unexplored. No details regarding the childhood sexual abuse were elicited, only a focus on what was useful in relation to dealing with the current impact of the abuse on Joyce's life, the therapist embedding a suggestion that Joyce continue doing what seemed to be useful to her. Similarly, no details of the past marital difficulties or of the current relationship with mother were sought. Perhaps in an analogous manner to psychoanalytic patients who learn to remember their dreams more and whose dreams slowly move towards accommodation with the interpretive orientation of the therapist, Joyce and David increasingly produced solution-talk and hence problem-talk diminished. The therapist's script, looking for exceptions, brought into relief for Joyce over a period of time a set of behaviours and attitudes which contradicted the problem pattern and a new and more complex pattern developed which contained within it solutions and control. As this pattern emerges into prominence the new script increasingly replaces the old and Joyce is envisaging a future in which she can both stand up for herself and be liked, indeed she produces a frame in which the two are linked. Without ever overtly dealing with the sexual abuse or the depression Joyce is able within three sessions to make increasingly confident strides to a different future.

CHAPTER FOUR

THE WRIGHT SORT OF MOTHER: A STATUTORY CASE

Mrs. Wright and her son John, both white, were referred by a Social Services Department. It was initially unclear whether the request was for assessment or treatment. Though the referrer came down in favour of treatment, there was a sense of lingering doubt. Given the circumstances which led to the referral this ambivalence was not surprising.

Mrs. Wright was twenty-eight and until three years previously had been in a sexual relationship with her father since early childhood. John's paternity was unclear. Aged ten, he was the subject of a supervision order to the Local Authority. Mrs. Wright's care of her son had been of much concern over several years and she had always relied on her parents for help. Five years previously she had had a second child, was kept in hospital herself due to an infection and on her discharge found the baby and its father had 'disappeared'. She has never seen either of them since.

Mrs. Wright's care of her son and of herself deteriorated sharply at this point. A period of struggle and decline culminated in her arrest for shoplifting and subsequent two-year imprisonment. John went to stay with his grandparents.

On release from prison Mrs. Wright tried to take over care of her son. Her parents opposed this, Social Services were involved and found much lacking in Mrs. Wright's parental ability. The matter went to Juvenile Court with the local Authority seeking a care order. The local Authority's case was upheld but the court decided John's best interest was still to live with his mother and a supervision order was made.

At this point a new social worker took over and as he had not been involved in the attempt to keep John from his mother he was more sympathetic to Mrs. Wright and wanted to give her the best chance. He had been working with her for a number of months and at the time of the referral had reached an impasse.

Few families can present with such an array of major trauma: abuse, incest, loss of a child, imprisonment and near loss of another child. Many therapists would wish to explore these events and even regard such exploration as a necessary part of treatment. With solution focused therapy, however, the field of discussion is largely client determined and therefore only those areas and events which the client considers relevant are open to exploration. A solution focus, therefore, challenges the view that past difficulties need to be understood or 'worked' through in order to solve current problems. Instead it offers an alternative – an interest in what has worked in the past, what is working in the present and what will work in the future. Handling the loss of a child without going completely mad is a potentially more healing notion than that of delinquency as a result of unresolved grief. So while listening to the client's story the therapist will be offering new viewpoints, some of which will challenge the negativity of the client's account.

THE FIRST SESSION

Mrs. Wright's particular circumstances – coming to a clinic because a powerful Social Services Department has suggested it – provide an excellent launch base for the beginning of some solution talk. Her obvious reluctance is a clear sign of her independence and readiness to fight while her presence is an equally clear sign of her ability to compromise when necessary, or even an indication that she will leave no stone unturned. Mrs. Wright had the added advantage of having won her court battle with Social Services.

By selecting these successful aspects of Mrs. Wright's account of her route to the clinic, her story is already in the process of being re-written:

Mrs. Wright: I just rebelled about everything which was happening round me.

Therapist: So you've come here with things already on the up and I suppose you and Mick *(the Social Worker)* have talked about it and want to find ways to keep it improving or speed it up a bit – you've already turned the boat round, as it were, and you're already going in the direction you want to go in.

W   Yeah.

T   That's terrific – so where, where do you want to go to so you can feel coming here was alright and you don't need to come any more?

By carefully listening to Mrs. Wright's story, showing special interest in areas of success, and by highlighting all signs of movement, Mrs. Wright's image of herself as a strong capable independent woman is enhanced at the expense of all those negative markers for which a woman in the 'welfare' limelight is a target. Within this early established context of movement, goal setting becomes a natural and logical step – 'you are on the move – where are you going?'

Mrs. Wright defines the problem in a way which makes the goal of therapy totally clear.

W At the moment I feel – there needs to be something stronger between me and John. At the moment he doesn't feel like he's mine. I don't know if you can understand that?

T Uhmm.

W He doesn't feel like he's mine – I mean…

Mrs. Wright has defined the problem in her terms and by implication the goal of therapy, which must be for her to feel like John *is* her child. The following sequence shows the therapist and client searching for a common foothold on this vague but pervasive problem.

The therapist first attempts to reduce the size of the problem, to bring it within the bounds of the 'normal'. Mrs. Wright does not find this helpful! The therapist tries to return to the concept of movement – that it is something that is already starting to happen. This too is rebuffed. Mrs. Wright is not going to have her own account, terrible as it is for her, so easily edited. Two small 'edits' are accepted, however. The first is to switch the problem from 'not feeling he's mine' to 'not feeling motherly' (and so putting it more within her own agency), and the second is to have it (at least temporarily) defined as a problem of 'patience'.

T Uhmm. Does he feel like someone else's, or his own or…

W I know from the time I was away it was like my Mum and Dad took over – it's…

T Right – so he feels like your Mum and Dad's.

W Yes.

T I think that's very natural, from what you've been through. They did take him over from you, they did teach him new ways.

W Yes.

T It was a struggle to get him back and, you know, an awful time for you to go through.

W Yes.

T But neither would it surprise me to find that in a month's time he would feel more like yours, and in three months' time that he feels even more like yours, because you're already -

W Yeah, but how's that going to happen – how's it going to happen?

T Well it sounds as if it's already started to happen. You know, your being – um – like it's, it sounds as if it's already started to happen and you just want it to happen a bit more.

W It seems like -

T How much is he yours at the moment? If you were going to put a percentage on it how much is he yours now, what per cent?

W   It's like – what I'm trying to say – you know like some mums, they put their arms round their kids and cuddle. When he comes for me to do that I can't. I sort of pull back, I -

T   Right.

W   I can't. I don't want it. And I don't know why.

T   So just from the little I've seen of you today you're very much like mother and son so you obviously feel a mother to him in some ways.

W   Oh yeah, I know. I'm a mother. I just feel that I'm not a *good* mother. You know what I mean?

T   But you're – from the little bit I've seen of you, you behave like a good mother as well as whatever else you do – and I haven't seen the other things.

W   Mmm.

T   But there's nothing wrong with what I've seen so far – so obviously you're not entirely – you're not a hundred per cent the wrong sort of mother.

W   No, but when he comes in and shows me something I feel...

T   Impatient.

W   Yeah, like I've got no patience – I just – I don't know, you know. The sort of things I should be doing with him -

T   So when, when is it different? When are the times when you do feel you've got some patience? When do you feel okay being close to him? When do these times happen?

W   They don't really.

The therapist almost loses Mrs. Wright on a number of occasions but hangs on to a belief that there must be exceptions for Mrs. Wright to have fought so hard for her son. But as each challenge to the story is rebuffed the therapist begins to feel desperate and it is this desperation which makes him think of his own children and asks, 'What about when he's asleep?' This proves to be the 'difference' which will eventually make a difference and from this point on Mrs. Wright seemed more engaged. This is not to say that she doesn't struggle to maintain her original story but she is also interested in the new one and so allows the therapist to interrupt and block her old account as they re-write a new account together. The aim now is to spend as long as possible on this episode, partly to extend the time spent in 'solution talk' but also to establish the event as one of prime significance – the discovery of an unnoticed treasure!

T   Uh hmm. What about when he's asleep -

W (Thoughtfully) Yeah. When he's asleep.

T Uhmm, what's he like when he's asleep?

W When he's asleep, sometimes I cry when he's asleep.

T Yes – you mean just looking at him.

W And I think why – why have I put him through this and why am I the way I am and -

T How close do you get to him when he's asleep and you're looking at him?

W I go over to him.

T How close do you get?

W Just by his bed – he's got one of those cabin beds you know.

T So how far away from his face will your face be?

W Like it is now I suppose (they are about four feet apart).

T Would you get closer to him than you are now when he's asleep?

W I sort of go over to him and kiss him when he's asleep – but I've got to wait until he's asleep and -

T So actually when he's asleep you get skin to skin.

W Yeah, but I've got to wait until -

T Does he know that? Has he ever woken up and caught you?

W No. (laughing)

T (To John) Have you secretly caught her – did you know she does this?

J One time when I was at Grandad's I opened my eyes and saw her kissing me.

T Did you – so you know that this goes on when you're asleep?

J Yes, but not when we've been living together.

T So you haven't opened your eyes and seen your Mum's face with tears in her eyes.

W (laughing) But he's seen me before with tears in my eyes.

T But not tears of love, looking at him.

W Uhmm.

T OK, so when he's asleep your tender motherly feelings start popping out.

W Yes, all those things. But only when he's asleep.

So the spell is broken – Mrs. Wright has intense motherly feelings and they have been incorporated into her account of her relationship with John. Though she still sees them as appearing 'only when he's asleep', it is a safe bet to assume they exist elsewhere too, and the therapist pushes on looking for other exceptions. It should be said that the discovery of this first exception and its amplification was a highly charged emotional experience for both Mrs. Wright and the therapist and by now they have developed immense trust in one another. Three more exceptions suddenly materialise – one noticed by the therapist, one by Mrs Wright and one by the almost forgotten John!

T   OK. So what about when he wakes up, first thing in the morning, what's he like then?

W   *(laughing a lot, as is John)* 'Orrible!

T   There's another very nice motherly thing – isn't it? You've obviously both got a sense of humour.

(A light-hearted discussion then follows about getting John off to school which the therapist compares with the morning shouting in his own family).

W   But I don't hit him!

T   No.

W   And I do everything that needs to be done before I go out to work in the morning.

T   What do you work at?

W   I'm a clerical typist at a big sports centre. My Mum got me a job there. Part-time.

T   So you work with your Mum?

W   No my Mum's in the Personnel Department. I'm in a different department.

T   Sorry, let's just go back. I took you away from what you were talking about the sort of – exceptions. When you do feel like a mum. And obviously, when he's asleep your tenderness, your motherly tenderness comes out; and when you think about the mornings and how you row in the mornings your motherly humour comes out and you laugh together.

W   Uhmm.

T   What are other times when your motherly feelings come out?

W   Uhmm. Well something that I've done, like his room for instance when we moved. I had people in to do this part and people in to do that. But when it came to John's room I done it all myself.

T   Did you?

W   Yeah, like papered it and decorated it.

T   That's what's called a 'labour of love' isn't it? That's what the expression means – doing something for love, doing something for someone special.

W   Well, I just wouldn't let no one- he knows *(pointing to John)* I wouldn't let no one go in or do anything to his room. Like my boyfriend wanted to do the wall papering – no, I wouldn't let no one do it.

T   So when it came to the bedroom he was one hundred per cent your son.

W   Yeah.

T   Right – so he's a hundred per cent your son while you cry while you look at him sleeping, he's a hundred per cent your son when you decorate his bedroom and I guess there are lots of other things like that. And he looked pretty well a hundred per cent your son when you laughed about how you are in the mornings, so there's a – I guess there's going to be – do you mind if I just ask John what he's noticed? Obviously you can't notice when you're asleep, but what have you noticed?

J   Sometimes when my Mum cries and she's upset she cuddles me; she tells me to 'come here' and she cuddles me.

T   So she *can* cuddle you.

J   Yeah, sometimes she pulls my hair back like this (*demonstrating a stroking motion*).

T   Do you like that – is it nice?

J   Yes.

T   Do you prefer the back of your head rubbed or the front?

J   I don't mind.

T   You like them both?

J   Yes (*laughter*).

T   I prefer the back myself.

W   (*to John laughing*). Are you sure you don't mean a smack on the back of your head?

In some circumstances, this last exception – John cuddling his mother – might have been ignored because it could be seen as evidence of the problem (a parent putting her needs before her child's). However, the therapist thought it had more weight as evidence of motherly capacities and, therefore, chose to emphasise that aspect of the cuddling.

And so this first part of the session ended with the client defined as on the way up even before therapy started, a clear problem, four powerful exceptions to the problem, and a goal.

It is a recurring discovery in our work that people who have faced great difficulties in their lives have strengths we would be proud to own ourselves. This is no more true than for women who have been sexually abused as children. It is almost as common for these strengths to go unrecognised – by the clients themselves and by those associated with them. Such clients are often said to have low self-esteem. Our own observation is that they are esteem blind – they have immense strengths developed to combat the most destructive of assaults on body and mind, they know they have these strengths but have somehow become blind to that knowledge. Mrs. Wright knew that she loved her son but had become blind to that knowledge. Once she regained her vision she had to reconstruct her past into one in which her love for her son was evident. The team, and the therapist, wanted to give feedback that would enhance and promote this rewriting of the past because it was exactly a rewritten past which would lead to the hoped for future. They were also wanting to emphasise the sense of movement but without imposing their own sense of direction (Mrs. Wright had been the subject of other people's wishes most of her life). Sometimes when giving feedback we will barely mention the 'problem' side of the equation at all, but with Mrs. Wright it seemed important to acknowledge her ordeals before moving on to her achievements.

T   We've been struck by a number of things and the thing which can't be avoided and must be taken very seriously is the number of terribly painful experiences you've been through – losing a child, imprisonment, abuse – all these things yet you're – you're obviously a person who's survived them.

W   Mmm.

T   And survived them with strength and with – you must be quite a person to have come through those and be here talking about them and being as strong as you are and that's something which is very very plain to everyone.

W   That's not the half of it there, either.

T   I'm sure it isn't. I'm sure it isn't. But even the little bit you've told us gives us a window on a pretty horrendous experience.

W   Mmm.

T   So you're quite a person to have come through that and to be as open as you've been with us. I'm also struck by your modesty – your modesty about yourself and your humility – playing down your strengths, playing down your achievements, your qualities, which is an unusual trait today.

W   Mmm (*agreeing*).

T   Modesty is a bit out of fashion at the moment. In fact, one of my colleagues was saying just now that deep down this woman has quite a fountain of love and (*to John*) you may not see it when you're asleep but one day it's going to be out there for everybody to see. We're also impressed with what you've managed to achieve, to still allow them to have the relationship that they have with your son, it's just incredible that you have the strength to do that. So, having said all that we'd like to offer you another appointment. We don't want to make it too soon because we've seen so much obvious development from what you've told us. And I'd like you to do some homework in between.

W   What's that?

The vagueness of this feedback is probably one of the reasons for Mrs. Wright being able to accept it as whole-heartedly as she did – that and the evidence collected during the session. Her response to the suggestion of a task, however, shows that she remains on guard. If necessary her suspicion can be used as evidence of her strength in resisting professionals – a wise philosophy in her vulnerable circumstances, but as it happens she becomes interested in the task and decides to consider it.

T   Both of you. It's about motherliness. You said you had no motherliness and then we found lots of motherliness. So I want to put it in an odd sort of way but I think it will be helpful to us when we next meet. If you were to score your motherliness and 10 was to be no motherliness at all and 1 was to be perfect motherliness, where would you score yourself now?

W   (After a long pause) About 6.

T   About 6 so almost half way to being a perfect mother. Good. And where would you be satisfied with reaching?

W   1.

T   Would you be satisfied with 1-to-2, or even 2?

W   Yes, but I'd aim for 1.

The 'problem' had now been shifted from no motherly feelings at all (which would have scored 10) to the need for a 40% change – from 6 to 2. It had therefore become not only manageable but almost half achieved already.

T   So you'd aim for 1 but settle for 2. OK. So look, I don't think I need to say go slowly because that's obvious, so what I'd like you to do between now and when we next meet – and you can both do it separately without conferring – what I'd like you to do, each evening, just for a minute or two, is to think about the day you've just had and remember all the times when you scored a 5.

This task (de Shazer et al, 1986) suggests everything and nothing. It implies the inevitability of change in exactly the direction the client wishes, yet it makes no attempt to define that direction or say what this interim goal – 5 – means in terms of action. That is left to the client.

THE SECOND SESSION

Our starting point for each session is to assume the problem is receding and the client's life improving. This is often enough the case for our stance to be reasonable. We also start from where we left off previously.

T   So what number 5s did you find yourselves doing then?

W   Do you mean how we've been?

T   Yes – tell me about some of the number 5s.

W   There's been about five of them.

T   Five! Tell me about them. Tell me about one of them. *(Mrs. W and John start to giggle).*

T   Is this one of them – when you get the giggles together?

W   One of them.

T   Or is that a number 4?

J   There's been a lot of number 4s.

T   What you mean, giggling a lot?

J   Yes. We laughed a lot more and things. And not arguing so much.

T   Tell me some more 5s then. Have you been watching him when he's asleep some more?

W   No.

T   You don't need to do that any more. You wait until he's awake now?

W   In case he wakes up and sees me so I don't do that no more.

T   What would you do if he did?

W   I don't know – you see in my eyes not a lot has changed.

T   So tell me about the number 5s – you said you could remember five of them so tell me about another one.

W   Five of them – laughing – I can't remember. I don't think there's been any change really except laughing and mucking about.

T   Right.

The therapist is not at this stage too worried about Mrs. Wright's sudden denial of change. The evidence before his eyes suggests otherwise, as does the initial response to the opening question. At this point it is safest to assume that Mrs. Wright is hanging on to her original story – not yet convinced that sufficient evidence exists to change it.

The session then continues in a similar vein to the first session in so far as Mrs. Wright raises a number of examples of her 'lack of motherliness' and then with a little encouragement produces exceptions to each of these. She has clearly been working very hard at establishing a different sort of relationship with her son, but characteristically has been at least ten times more aware of the set-backs than she has of her achievements.

Of particular significance was a reduction in contact between Mrs. Wright and her parents (the referrer saw this as evidence of growing independence and parental autonomy), and within the mother-son relationship a new negotiating style had been developed. They were working out a way of living together by bargaining over almost every issue. This was clearly giving them great pleasure and taking up a great deal of their time! The improved quality of their relationship as they talked, laughed and argued together was obvious to everyone throughout the session. But Mrs. Wright could not see this. Instead she saw one unsuccessful bargain and this continued to prove her a 'bad' mother.

The relentless blowing of someone else's trumpet may seem boring to some therapists, patronising or even embarrassing to others; it is nevertheless an extremely effective way of getting the trumpet-owners to reclaim their instrument and show them how it really should be played. At the break in the second session the therapist was encouraged to hand it back!

T   Things are going pretty well and the team couldn't see any reason for you to be here because from what they can see things are going pretty well.

W   Uhmm.

T   We only usually see people who are pretty desperate. And they were very struck by your determination. They loved it when you said you were going to get it [a car] and Mick said you'd need a licence and then you said 'and I'm bloody well going to get it'.

W   *(laughing)* Yeah!

T   Because that seems to characterise you – that's the sort of person you seem to be. You've got something in mind and -

W   Yeah – if I aim for something, I get it.

T   And you're going to get it. So you're aiming for a good relationship with your son -

W   Then I'll have it. I'll have it whether it's with the help from you or the help from – but I'll have it, it'll just come.

This is a powerful trumpet blast but is followed in the same breath by one of Mrs. Wright's last attempts to hang on to her old story. It in fact leads to some delicate finger play and the therapist letting go.

W   But what I'd like to point out before I forget it. You see me and John in front of you now and I'm not saying it's a front or anything like that, I'm not saying that. It's just like if you were able to see the way I sometimes react I don't think personally it's John who needs help, it's me.

T   I think you've given us a very good picture of how you react. I know we've only seen a little of you but you've told us a lot. In fact you've been very open – very open with the things that worry and trouble you. But the other thing is that each time you've come up with one you've also come up with an answer.

W   Mmm.

T   You've also come up with the ideas in your head already about how to make it better.

W   Mmm.

T   And the business about you doing something that he wants and he doing something that you want, and bargaining – you've already started the bargaining and the only slight change that might be necessary is to make sure that he does his bit first so – because you know you'll do your bit.

W   But then I might not necessarily do my bit.

T   Well, you seem experienced and mature enough to, even if you don't like to do it, to do it.

W   It's like a few weeks ago I said, right I'm not biting my nails no more. I've bitten my nails all my life. All of a sudden I've stopped biting them and I grew them just like that.

T   And you're telling me you can't do something like look at a book of his if you say you're going to.

With such progress a longer interval is made before the next session for the explicit purpose of minimising the therapist's interference ('When things are going so well we don't like to interfere.')

In thinking about a task, de Shazer suggests repeating any earlier task that worked. The scaling task, 'look out for the 5s at the end of their first session had certainly been followed by significant changes, and the second session task might simply have been 'Now look out for some more 4s'. However, the therapist wished to incorporate the family's independently developed solution – the bargaining process. To this end he helps them re-negotiate the failed bargain – she to look at his homework and he to go walking with his mother. Each is then asked to 'look out for the 4s' while they are doing the activity they dislike – he walking, she looking at his work.

THE THIRD SESSION

T   How did you get on with all the things you were going to do?

W   *(laughing)* We did a lot of walking!

T   How was that John, how did you score that?

J   Nine out of ten. *(They have both reversed the scaling order)*

T   Nine out of ten! How about you, you were going to look at some books?

W   Mmm.

T   How did you rate that?

W   About eight, maybe nine out of ten.

T   So how did you like that – did you like your Mum looking at your work?

J   Yeah.

W   His work's very neat. Very very neat.

The successful accomplishment of this task had finally convinced Mrs. Wright that a new pattern had been established. As the session progressed and her successes were reviewed her questioning of the 'new order' virtually disappeared. John however remained on the Child Protection Register and was still subject to a supervision order. As the local Authority Social Worker was present throughout the meetings, an ideal opportunity was available for Mrs. Wright to see her successes reflected in Social Services action. The Social Worker was extremely close to Mrs. Wright ('He's the only person who visits my house'), but was also acting on behalf of the Authority which was naturally dubious about this rapid transformation of the family's behaviour and presentation. The therapist challenged both Mrs. Wright and the Social Worker: Mrs. Wright to demand recognition of the changes and the Social Worker to give recognition, not just with words but also by action.

At the final and fourth session some two months later and some five months after the first meeting, Mrs. Wright had moved from a new temporary part-time clerical position to a full-time office supervisor post, she had ceased entirely to depend on her parents for practical or emotional support and had just passed her driving test. John was attending school (which he had not been doing) and had a more robust appearance and manner. His name was no longer on the Child Protection Register and the Social Worker was arguing the case for an early return to Court and the rescinding of the Supervision Order.

COMMENT

Within the terms of the model, an explanation of the dramatic changes is simple: the client was already moving and the therapy simply added a little to the momentum. What it did not do, however, was to interrupt the movement in order to 'examine the engine'! The most important plus to Mrs. Wright was the discovery of her tears. After that the exceptions came so thick and fast it was necessary to remember to keep asking for them. With such a process it was inevitable that Mrs. Wright's 'problem' would collapse under the accumulated weight of its exceptions.

CHAPTER FIVE

THE WOMAN WHO THOUGHT SHE WAS WEAK
School Non-Attendance

'Could I ask that you are fairly gentle in view of father's reluctance to be involved (using video will truly put the family off)', wrote the referring Educational Psychologist. Having said that, she asked for the Clinic's help with Steven, aged 14, in his third year at secondary school, who had truanted consistently for one whole term, attending school not at all during that time, and whose school attendance had been increasingly sporadic during his whole second year. Steven's difficulties with school had led the Education Department to begin an assessment of his Special Educational Needs and the Clinic was asked to contribute towards this assessment as well as 'possibly' to offer 'counselling'.

Steven, a white boy, the younger of two with an older brother of 19 who had left home, was living with his white mother and father. Steven's mother had been diagnosed some years earlier as having multiple sclerosis but was in remission at the time of referral.

FIRST SCHOOL MEETING

Although at the time of referral Steven's total absence from schooling meant that the school was not involved with him and his family, any solution to the problem would depend, in part, on the Education Department's view. So to check out what educational resources might be available to Steven as part of the solution, a meeting at the school was arranged, and attended by the referrer, the Education Social Worker, the School Year Head, the family and by the Clinic Therapist. The family was represented by mother, Carol Roberts, her sister Wendy and Steven.

The meeting kicked off with Carol saying to the referrer, 'He wouldn't come – I knew he wouldn't.' Carol was referring to her husband. Everyone knew that. No one was surprised. She added that Wendy was there as her 'memory' – 'since the MS, it's difficult for me to remember things and to say what I mean.' Was anything much expected from her or had everyone bought the idea that not a lot could be hoped for? Did Carol see herself as potentially competent or as a disabled person whom others had to support?

Three possibilities were put forward for Steven and his education – either a return to his current school, where he was still on roll despite his truancy, or a transfer to a new school, or Home Tuition. Questioning both family and professionals around these options excluded the Home Tuition. It was recognised that this would not make enough of his potential. But the question of 'which school' was more difficult. Not only was it more difficult but it was not clear who would decide, as mother and aunt anxiously talked with Steven about what he thought would be best.

Steven was not bothered much anyway. In school he reckoned he was 'persecuted'. The Year Head agreed that Steven got into trouble with teachers, but stated that he regularly made trouble, and would not accept being told off. Staying at home and watching TV was all right with Steven. Here was no customer for change! But Carol Roberts did have a goal. She wanted Steven back in school, even though she did not know which school; but she took the view, supported by her sister Wendy, that there was nothing she could do to get Steven back. He would have to make up his own mind, they thought. Steven would have to make the change.

Offering a further appointment, two venues were put forward, either home or clinic. Would father, Trevor, be more likely to see the therapist in his own home? Carol thought not and opted for the clinic. Before finishing, Carol was asked just to notice anything that happened that was different between that meeting and the first clinic session.

FIRST CLINIC SESSION

Sensitive to the Referrer's injunction proscribing video, the family was seen in an office without screen, without video and without team. Carol Roberts had come with Wendy again, but had decided not to bring Steven. Trevor, she said, had not wanted to come.

During the two week interval, Carol had noticed some differences, mainly that Steven had gone back to school for four whole days and two half days. Neither Carol nor Wendy had any explanation for this. He had gone, they thought, because he had decided to; he had run out twice because he was being 'persecuted', he said, and he had stopped again, altogether, equally mysteriously. The school staff confirmed that Steven had got into trouble and had run out of school. Carol had noted changes but no exceptions, it seemed, to the family's idea that Steven only attended school if he chose. Not only were there no exceptions in the recent past according to mother and aunt, but in the more distant past Carol had never been able to get him to go in if he was minded against it. Moving on to the older son produced nothing different. He had never truanted once, but then 'he had loved school'. Broadening the enquiry in the search for exceptions, the therapist enquired, 'Tell me about the times you get Steven to do the things that you want him to do that he doesn't want to do.' 'Never,' it seemed, was the answer to this, and Carol and Wendy began to produce strings of examples of how Steven got his own way, with Wendy adding that Steven 'never listens – he shows no respect'. Continuing to search for exceptions- 'How does Steven show his respect for you [Carol]'- led to more of the same. Wendy and Carol's view was that he never did, 'just like his father'. Wendy explained protectively, that Trevor had never been any help to Carol in bringing up Steven and David and that the family had spent years trying to get Carol to leave him. She had, a few times, but always went back. 'Do you want your son to grow up like Trevor?' 'No, absolutely not.'

After taking a break to consult with himself the therapist proceeded to compliment Carol on Steven's return to school 'for a number of days for the first time for months', and to comment on her strength: her strength in resisting her family's pressure to leave Trevor; her strength in bringing up two children virtually single-handed; and the strength of her determination to get for Steven everything she thought he should have (the previous year she had spent £250, which she did not have, on a model car that Steven had wanted). Finally a linked pair of tasks were prescribed. Carol was asked to notice what was different about the times that Steven did what she wanted, with the implicit suggestion that there would be such times, and she was asked 'to do something different'. 'Steven thinks he's got you all taped, that you're all under his thumb – shake him up a bit, do something different.'

Right at the end of the session the therapist said 'I want to do something different next time as well... normally I work with a team who are there to help me to help you. Next time I want to see you with my team. OK?' It was fine with Carol.

SECOND CLINIC SESSION

Carol came back to the clinic with Wendy one week later. Yet again, she declined to bring Steven. The intervening period had been school half-term. Two minutes in, after Carol had said 'Hi' to the team through the screen and '1, 2, 3 testing' to the microphone in the middle of the room, the therapist starts off:

Therapist: What's been happening different since last we met?
Carol: Well, I tried with Steven what you said, 'Notice what's different

when Steven does what you want him to do and do something different.' Well... I've been doing things very differently.

T   Have you? That's great. *(to Wendy)* Have you noticed this?

Wendy: I haven't been around actually.

The fact that Wendy had not been around was different in itself and would be useful to come back to, but it was more important to return to Carol.

T   So you've been doing things differently on your own?

C   Yes.

T   So what is it that you've been doing differently?

C   I've been putting my foot down and saying 'No' all the time. *(She laughs anxiously)*.

T   Have you? Was it that dreadful or was it...?

C   Well, I'm not used to hearing myself saying 'No' and he [Steven] kept on and on. 'Please can I do it?' 'No'. Then he'd go away with the hump, put himself in his room for ten minutes and come back. 'Can I?' 'No, Steven. It's not necessary, you can't do it.' 'Well I'm not going to school.'

T   So he was threatening you.

C   And 'I'm not going to do this, that and the other' and I said 'Please yourself, it's still no...'

T   Great.

C   He's [Steven] been very... *(to Wendy)* what did I say to you, helpful. Like if I let him go out and he's over his friends he says 'Shall I take the dog down?' 'No. The dog's already been down.'

T   But that's something that you said last time that Steven would create a huge stink about taking the dog down or doing something for you.

C   Yes. Because I'm so determined in what I've been doing over the last few days, he's changing as well. I got to keep this up so that's...

T   OK. What's it been like for you?

C   Great. It's been absolutely great. I'm thinking I'm in control not only of myself but my son. I'm just wondering with the start back to school on Monday the approach to have on that because his friend...

At this point the therapist notes that Carol is about to move away from her successes to uncertainties about how to handle the question of school in the future. In order to build a firmer and more confident basis for exploring uncertain future issues, in relation to which Carol had in the last session been able to generate no 'exceptions', the therapist wants her to experience and explore her success – unusual and new for her – more fully.

T   Tell me a bit more about the things that you've been doing. Let's not rush over it. Let's enjoy it. What sort of things?

C   Things like he wanted to stay over his friend's across the road because his friend was baby-sitting there and I said, 'No, you're only across the road. It's not necessary.'

T   OK.

C   You can stay out to 11.00 but then be back.

T   In the past would you have said 'Yes' to that? You'd have said 'Yes' before.

While introducing the past in this way can bring the client's 'failure' back into therapy, raising it in the context of a different sort of behaviour in the present serves to focus and to amplify the change.

C   Would I have said 'yes'?

T   Yes.

C   Oh yes. I'd have said 'OK. Steven'.

T   Even though you weren't really terribly happy and didn't think that it was necessary?

C   Yeah. I wasn't happy about it at the time but I'd have still said 'yes'.

T   Right, so now you said what you really meant and what you really wanted this time.

The therapist fetes the changes in a way that develops the rapport between client and therapist (Lipchick and de Shazer 1986) and stabilises the basis for the next step. Another way of amplifying the change is to explore it with the client, through the eyes of others:

T   Steven's obviously noticed a change.

C   I think he must have done…

T   If he's beginning to behave differently then that suggests that somewhere he's noticed a change. What's he doing differently? So he actually offered to take the dog for a walk?

C   Yes. Came in at 10 to 11, instead of 11 and said, 'Oh, shall I take the dog down?' 'Can I sit and watch the film with you?' 'Yes, but you're not watching all of it. I'll tape it and you can watch it tomorrow.'

T   And he stuck to that did he?

C   Yes he stuck to it. It's normally an argument. 'Well, I'll watch it in bed then… I'll go to bed and watch it.' But I didn't get any of that, and talking about holidays I said, 'Things have got to change. If you're going on holiday then you help me. We can save some money and we can have a holiday. I'll help you but you can't keep taking money from me every day and still expect to go on holiday at the end of the year.'

T   Right, whereas normally you'd have scrimped and saved and made it happen somehow.

C   Yes.

T   I remember you telling me about the car that you made happen somehow…

C   Yes. I normally make everything happen. But this time…

T   Does that mean that you're not going to make quite so much happen… everything that Steven wants?

C   Yes I will. Yes definitely because I can see that I can do it. I can say 'No' and mean it.

T   OK. Do you think that Steven's Dad has seen the difference? I know that he's not around much.

C   No. He's not there to see it.

T   He's not there to see it at all? So one day when he spots it he's going to have a big surprise is he?

The 'other person perspective' questions which follow, aim to embed Carol's different and new view of herself by concentrating on how other family members will perceive the difference in Carol.

T   Steven's Dad at some point, we're not sure how soon, but at some point is going to notice that he's more polite, that Steven's more polite?

C   Yes.

T   What do you think he'll think when he notices that?

T   Do you think Wendy would be the person who'd notice most in your family or would there be other members who might notice?

C   Wendy.

T   (to Wendy) You'll be the first one to spot the change will you?

W   Yes. I think so. I'm with her all the time.

T   Yes. You're most around, you're most in touch, you know what's going on. OK, who do you think will be next to spot the change in your family?

C   No one really. Who else?… I don't know.

T   Who'll notice that things are different? What about… How many sisters are you? Three?

C   Three.

T   What about your other sister?

C   No, because she does her own work. She's hardly ever around.

T   OK, so you've got brothers?

C   Three brothers. They're working all the time. I suppose it'll be my Mum.

T   OK. So what's your Mum going to notice come the day she realises something different is going on?

W   His reactions to Carol because my Mum gets very uptight with Steven the way he acts with Carol... very annoyed.

T   So she'll notice it because it bothers her [Mum].

Carol has defined her goal as getting Steven back to school and in attempting to achieve this she has begun to say 'No'. Holding in mind the question of how this change will be maintained, the therapist begins to check out the wider systemic implications of this shift.

C   ...I often think that maybe it's Trevor, because he doesn't show me any [respect] that Steven thinks he can do the same thing probably. It's quite natural, isn't it ?

T   OK. So maybe he's copying Dad a bit and you were saying last week you don't want him to be like Dad.

C   No I don't.

T   OK. If you start saying 'No', you don't think it's going to start rubbing off on Trevor too do you?

C   (laughs) I don't know. You mean me saying 'No' to him, you mean...

T   I was just wondering whether Trevor was going to get a shock one day when you start not only saying 'No' to Steven when you mean 'No' but saying 'No' to Trevor when you mean 'No'.

C   I don't know.

W   You have said 'No' to Trevor, Carol.

T   Oh, you have?

C   Yes, but only for trivial little things.

W   He takes no notice anyway.

T   OK, but you see Steven didn't used to take any notice – he used to push and push and push until you...

C   Gave in.

T   So Steven's beginning to experience something different... but you're not here about Trevor... that's something else.

C   (laughs).

T   OK.

C   I'm determined I'm not going to be the 'Yes Yes Yes' person. I've mostly thought about what you said to me and it came across very, very strongly... this has obviously got to do Steven a hell of a lot of good and myself in the meantime.

T   What's going to keep you going?

Carol discusses with the therapist how her sister Wendy and her mother will both support her and keep her to task, before adding that it is the changes that she sees in her son that will be her greatest encouragement. Sensing a danger of disillusionment should Steven's progress not be smooth and regular, the therapist moves to deal with this.

C   I'm seeing such a difference in Steven. It'll make it a hell of a lot easier to think I'm not doing it and wasting my time.

T   I guess you realise this but with some children they start making a change and then they dig their heels in for a time and have a big fight and life gets more difficult and then things start getting better again and so, often, as things begin to change it's up and then maybe it drops a bit and then it continues going up... it's not always a smooth line getting better and better and better. So there's maybe a time that he'll dig his heels in and make you work even harder than you've had to work in this last week, you know.

C   Well... I'd have to do it. I'm definitely determined to keep this up and to see where it leads him.

W   In fact he threatened to leave home, didn't he...?

Wendy explains that Steven has already begun the 'big fight'. The highly attuned 'constructive ear' (Lipchik, 1988) that the therapist develops in solution focused work, and which listens for exceptions and successes, leads to an exploration of how Carol handled Steven's threat to 'leave home' differently on this occasion.

T   ...So you didn't get roused by it?

C   No. I thought, I can't. If he sees that I'm going to be that way he's going to do it all the more, so I kept that all in and thought very positively about it and...

T   Do you think it surprised him?

C   Yes. Because he thought 'What do I do now?' He just sat there and...

T   So the old tactics that have worked in the past didn't seem to be working.

C   He hasn't even asked me, 'Why are you being like this?' He seems to be going along with it. I don't understand it. It might be what he wants.

In other circumstances Carol's idea that her new firmness 'might be what he wants' may have been a useful one. Here, however, it is more important to focus on Carol getting what she wants, a major difference, rather than on developing a frame which might suggest that what Carol wants is really what Steven wants.

T   OK. So within five days you've begun to experience something different for yourself and saying 'No' and beginning to see something different with Steven... What else... what other times do you say 'No', apart from to Steven?

C   I've never really said 'No'.

T   What about to your sister?

C   Do I say 'No' to my sister? Not really. *(laughs)*... I never say 'No' to her... no.

T   You don't... and to your Mum?

C   I never say 'No' to her either.

W   We sort of help one another.

C   That's the way it's always been.

T   So what you're doing with Steven is pretty new, not just with Steven but in the family as a whole... because people in your family like to say 'Yes' to each other. Is that right?

W   Yeah. Basically.

T   So most of the time you like to say 'Yes' if you possibly can.

C   Don't like to hurt anybody.

W   We help one another.

T   So the idea that it might be helpful to Steven to say 'No' is sort of different... you *(to Wendy)* were saying that if it helps people to say 'Yes' you say 'Yes' but the idea that it might be useful to Steven to start saying 'No' is sort of different.
OK.
What... how do you see the next couple of weeks?

C   The same as those just gone I hope.

T   OK. What do you see yourself doing?

About twenty minutes after Carol first raises the issue of Steven's return to school after half-term, the therapist invites a dialogue about the subject on a new and different footing, since now the question follows twenty minutes of change talk (Gingerich et al, 1987), during which time differences, exceptions and successes have been noted and discussed in detail.

C   I've got no idea what's going to happen on Monday morning... and I don't know how to react on that, whether to say, 'You're not staying at home, you're going to school...' If I say that, I'm thinking he's going to walk the streets which he's done before so I don't know how to react on that one.

T   What thoughts have you had so far? Where's your thinking taking you? Because whatever you've done, you know, it's been very successful in this last week. I guess because you're the person, in some senses, who knows Steven best and so you've known how to judge things and how to get it right.

C   I haven't had any really good thoughts on it... I can't think of anything that's going to... without him thinking that I'm pushing him to go and it not coming from him to go to school on Monday. I don't know what to do to encourage this without being too abrupt.

T   Yes. What possibilities are there for you, do you think?

C   There was one. I've just remembered it. I did say to him he could get his friends involved in the fund-raising (for the local MS Society), and, if not his friends, maybe a few school-teachers. I thought maybe that'd get him to school.

T   So link him [Steven] into school in a different way.

C   Yeah. That was one.

T   What ideas are around? – because I guess it's not just you [Carol] thinking about school but the family as well. What [other] possibilities do you see?

C   None at the moment.

W   To get him back into school?

T   Yes.

W   Well, it's his own mind. That's the whole problem with Steven.

T   But, you see *(to Wendy)*, at the moment your sister is doing something that's having quite a dramatic effect on Steven's mind... what she's doing seems to be producing the beginnings of some respect and we don't know how far that's gone yet and its early days yet...

C   Very early.

T   In the sense that, as you *(to Wendy)* realise it's going to have to carry on of course, but something's beginning to happen to Steven's mind as your sister does something different... as he becomes more thoughtful and respectful as he should be.

The remainder of this session, until the team consulting break, produces no more ideas about how to get Steven back to school, nor any more direct exceptions from the past, although the overall context, in which mother has learned that she can be 'in control not only of myself but of my son', has shifted fundamentally. A useful idea that is pursued is the idea that mother's tougher attitude at home may help Steven to deal with experiences at school that he interprets as 'persecution' as he learns that in saying 'No', his mother is not 'persecuting' him.

Following the consulting break, the therapist returns with a set of compliments and an Implied suggestion for Carol. The compliments utilise an idea expressed during the interview. She refers to qualities lying dormant, just under the surface. Using this idea in relation to Steven, that he's a potentially co-operating, helpful boy, served to diminish mother's paralysing sense of guilt with reference to her idea of her past poor parenting. Similarly the therapist incorporated the idea in relation to her own behaviour. Facilitating dormant strengths would always be easier than creating something new. By referring to the support available from Carol's family, the therapist was aiming to address his perception of some tension between Wendy and Carol, as Carol is increasingly focused on her successes.

T   The first thing that we were talking about was just being extremely impressed by the way you've started saying 'No'. The way we were hearing it was that it was almost like the saying 'No' was just there under the surface waiting to be used, because once you started doing it, you've done it and it's happened and that's been fine. So it's like it's always been there, the possibility of saying 'No' but you haven't practised it and so what you've started doing is practising it. And we're very struck by that, you know, very struck both by the change that you've made and by, in some senses, how it's come to you without huge difficulty. Is that fair?

C   Yeah, very fair. I agree with it.

T   And we're struck by, in addition, how Steven has responded to that. He's responded with increased thoughtfulness and increased respect and although he's got some way to go down that road nonetheless the beginnings of it are there and what that meant for us was that it also was underneath the surface waiting to emerge. So clearly what's happened for Steven in his early years, till now, has helped him to be able to behave in a more respectful and more thoughtful way as soon as the context for that happened. So as soon as you started to do something that allowed that to happen then the behaviour's there and it starts emerging. So our guess is that whatever's happened to Steven has prepared him for this, that between you and the work that the rest of the family has done you've laid the groundwork for Steven to be a thoughtful and respectful young man, and what you've done is to provide the opportunity for him to express his thoughtfulness and respectfulness and particularly in relation to you.

C   Yeah (*Carol nods*).

T   That makes us hopeful. Obviously because if it had been a huge struggle for Steven to find respectful and thoughtful ways of behaving then it would have involved more work, but clearly it's there and it's just a question of helping to release that more thoughtful and respectful behaviour particularly in relation to you. Yes?

C   Yes.

T   What we're also very struck by is the absolute confidence you have that your family's around and can be relied upon to support you and that's very nice... there are lots of people who couldn't say that.

C   We're quite a close family... well I'd like to say we're very close... but I think what really set me off was you last week... I mean you said things to me that I didn't think of myself....

T   OK. sure but...

C   If this man can see this in me then it's obviously there...

T   Yeah, we were talking about the strength that you'd used.

C   And I thought I was quite a weak person and I used to think, 'No I can't do that' and when you actually came out with that to me, well he must know, he must see it in me, so I'm going by...

T   And when you tried it was there.

C   Yes.

T   OK, so maybe I was right (laughs).

C   I think so, yeah definitely, because I said to Wendy going out, you know I didn't expect the answers that I got from you about myself. I thought I was going to come here and tell you all that was happening and you're saying to me 'it's your fault, it's down to you... you shouldn't be the person that you are' and so forth and she said, 'No it's nothing like that, not at all.'

T   No.

C   And I thought 'Right I'll go ahead with this...'

T   ...and do it and you've done it.

W   I think you highlighted it.

C   Oh, definitely.

T   OK. So obviously that means that it was something that somewhere you were aware of but you needed someone else to notice.

The therapist attempts to minimise the part played by the therapy and to maximise the credit accruing to the client.

W   She's used to me saying to her, 'Carol you shouldn't do this,' but when it comes to an outsider that doesn't know her background saying, 'Well, what about you Carol? How do you feel about this?'

You said to her last time, 'Why do you always put yourself second?' is what you said to her

T   Yes.

W   Someone from not in the family to say that brought it to light.

C   It lifted it right out and I thought 'Oh'!

T   OK, let me just... the other thing I wanted to say was that what I heard from you, and we were talking about this last week as well, is that the persuading job of Steven that school's a good thing is done; he's fully persuaded that school's a good thing.

C   Oh yes.

T   And what he needs is tipping over into not just being persuaded but doing it. It's a bit like all those things were just ready under the surface waiting to come out and just a little tip and different things started to happen. So what we're looking for is a slightly different tip with Steven so that different things start to come about. Steven's already given us hints that this can happen because after all in the last week before half-term he did go back to school for a number of days. So he's told us that going back isn't impossible; it can be managed. What we're struck by is that what you've done this week is to be able to say 'No' to Steven outright. You've said 'No you're not going to do that' and he's bought that. OK? You've had to insist, sure, but he's bought it, you've felt your strength, you've experienced it and he's bought it. Of course what there is is a process from that to you saying 'Yes' to Steven, 'you will do what I expect'. It's just one line that goes from saying 'No you won't do that' to 'You won't do that, and you will do the other.' OK? It's like you were saying 'No you won't go and stay with your mate across the road and you will come home.' So what we predict you'll be doing more of over the next few weeks is moving through from saying 'No Steven you can't do that' to 'No Steven you can't do that and you will do this.' Alright?

C   OK. Yes.

T   We don't know how you're going to make that happen but we have every confidence that that's...

C   I'll have a good go.

T   ...what's going to happen and we'll look forward to meeting you in two weeks time to hear what happened. OK?

C   OK. Thank You (*Shakes hands*). Another step forward.

THIRD CLINIC SESSION

Carol rang the clinic the day before her next appointment, two weeks later, to cancel. She was unwell. The therapist rang back. Steven should have been back at school for eleven days by now. Carol seemed disappointed, but on enquiring she said it was because on a few occasions he had run out of school at 1.30p.m. When the therapist suggested that this must mean that Steven had been back in school some days, Carol answered, 'Yes, every day.' The pace of change was being maintained.

DISCUSSION

In some ways this referral might initially have seemed unpromising. Not only was the client unable to specify exceptions to the problem pattern but the problem was apparently constructed in such a way as to appear impervious to change:

> Steven doesn't go to school.
> Steven doesn't want to go to school.
> Steven only does what he wants.
> Carol doesn't believe that she can change Steven's mind.
> Carol believes that she has never got Steven to do what she wanted and he didn't want to do.

However, the compliments at the end of the first clinic session clearly diverged sharply from Carol's expectations regarding the process of therapy and acted as 'news of a difference' in relation to her view of herself. The change that subsequently occurs, 'I've been putting my foot down and saying "No" all the time,' leads Carol to say, 'I can see that I can do it. I can say "No" and mean it.' As this different view is exposed, amplified and built upon in the second clinic session, the divergence between Carol's pre-therapy view and her current experience is increased, the pace of change quickens and the treatment moves into a new stage – 'After the Miracle' (Kral and Kowalski, 1989). The task of therapy in this second stage is to find ways of maximising the likelihood that the process of change will continue. While making another appointment with the family the need for a further school-family meeting is agreed so that the change in the home context can be supported by the school.

CHAPTER SIX

BEST OF FIVE: An Eating Disorder

Miss Bonchance was a white woman aged 23. Her parents were French but lived in London where she was brought up. She lived and worked in France. She was referred by her GP because she had eaten no solids for three months, vomited up most of what she drank and was taking laxatives every day. She had experienced eating and weight difficulties since the age of 12 but this was her first referral for treatment. Miss Bonchance returned to her parents' London home on Sunday, saw her GP on Tuesday and (because of a cancellation) was seen by the team on Wednesday. By Monday she was eating normally and the following weekend, two weeks after her arrival, she returned to France.

THE FIRST SESSION

Miss Bonchance was very much distressed by her problem and very keen to find a resolution. The fact that she had managed to handle the problem for eleven years led the therapist to assume that she already had many successful ways of dealing with it. Finding what these were and building on them seemed a good way forward. The aim of this first session was therefore to 'tune her in' to her existing and potential solution patterns and join with her to expand them.

Therapist: Dr. E was saying that when you'd got too light or too heavy – I'm not sure which – in the past you'd done something about it before it had become a problem – what do you think she meant?

Miss Bonchance: I'm not sure actually because I don't remember seeing her about weight problems. I'd see her about other things and she'd weigh me. But it could have been – I've been like this from about 12 onwards – I think I did go for a diet.

T   So how have you kept it from being a problem for so long?

B   I never thought about it, I didn't feel it was important.

Like anyone coming for therapy Miss Bonchance needs to have her problem heard and several minutes are spent on this. Interesting information emerges which in other models may have become therapeutically significant. Miss Bonchance had lived in France for three years but frequently came to visit her parents. This current episode had begun towards the end of a month-long visit to her by her parents. When they returned to England she stopped eating. Her employer had persuaded her to return to London, when two and a half months later, she had lost two and a half stone and was beginning to look ill. Her parents had taken time off work to be with her at home and were preventing her vomiting and taking laxatives.

While the story is unfolding any opportunity to define the problem as solvable is taken.

T   So it was just like lots of women and some men who occasionally go on a diet – so it's been a fairly normal thing?

B   Yes.

T   And when did you see this new development starting?

B   It must have been the beginning of August or end of July.

T   And when did the vomiting start?

B   That was about six weeks ago.

T   So it's a very new development.

B   Yes, it is. I just got a bit scared when I tried to stop it, trying to stop going out and buying laxatives and I couldn't do it.

T   So it's a new development and you want to nip it in the bud.

At the same time the significance of the parents is being considered by the therapist and the team. The parents are actually sitting in the waiting room during this meeting, having brought their daughter to the clinic. Miss Bonchance had made it clear she did not want them involved in the session.

While problems are being defined the therapist needs to be on the lookout for opportunities to discover exceptions, or at least differences. Ten minutes into the session Miss Bonchance is describing how with her parents around she is 'kept busy'.

T   So while you're kept busy it's less of a problem?

B   I'm just kept busy really and I don't think about it but when I have to eat and I will eat...

T   When you say you 'have to' is that you or someone else saying you have to?

B   No, I feel I have to even though I don't want to feel I have to.

T   So you have quite a lot of self-control then?

In this short sequence an exception is highlighted and leads straight into another ingredient for solution building – self control – before returning to more problem talk. It is two or three minutes before another solution focus is accepted by the client.

T   So again, this is very new. So is it a surprise to you that you find yourself doing this?

B   Yes, I just seemed to fall into it. I don't recall how it happened or when was the first time or what made me do it, I just had this need to do it. I think it is that feeling emptier – not having anything in your stomach you feel better.

T   Right – so it makes you feel better? How long does it last for – feeling better?

B   Until you start feeling hungry or want to eat something.

T   What about if you make yourself vomit do you think 'Oh here I go again' or don't you get those feelings of regret that you've…

B   No I don't – it's awful because you have your good days and you have your bad. You have those days when you just don't want to do anything like that.

T   What makes a good day? What sort of things happen on a good day?

This last question is the turning point for the therapy. It is particularly significant because it has been introduced spontaneously by Miss Bonchance. The de Shazer team have developed a task based on a 'good days bad days' problem and it was this which guided the rest of the session, or almost! The therapist first gets pulled into more problem talk and even escalates this into a discussion about the ultimate effects of not eating. On this occasion it is the client who switches back into solution talk and prompts the therapist to get back to business.

T   Do you think you would have died in the end then?

B   I don't know, I think I wouldn't. I think I was a bit clever and admitted to it and seen someone rather than letting it carry on. Now it's just happened recently.

T   So you are actually somebody who picks up very quickly on a difficulty and decides to do something about it rather than letting it go on.

B   I think it depends on like what the problem is.

T   Yes.

B   But I knew that if I didn't see anyone I would just carry on because I just couldn't stop it – I couldn't stop it.

T   Tell me then. What do you think makes the difference between a good day and a bad day? What leads to it happening?

The answer to this crucial question comes out over the next five or six minutes with the most important question being 'What else…?'

T   OK, on a good day you might go window shopping. Go out for a walk, did you say?

B   Yes, I might go out for a newspaper or something. Just go down the road. I'll get as far as the park,

T   So you actually go in the park? So you get around quite a bit. What else will you be doing on a good day?

B   Watch a video. Uhmm…

T   Watch a video, yes. Do you go out to get a video or have you got a stock in?

B   I've just convinced my Mum to become a member so eventually I will go out.

T   So you'll go out. What else will you do on a good day?

This produces four activities (later joined by a fifth): window shopping, walking, watching videos and a future possibility of contacting friends. These will form the basis of the homework task. The fact that Miss Bonchance is unable to predict when a good day will happen is also taken into account in the construction of a task.

This key point has been reached in less than twenty-five minutes. What remains is to develop more specific goals and further explore Miss Bonchance's experiences of problem solving.

T   So when this problem starts to disappear what are the first things you are likely to notice happening?

B   I've got an appetite.

T   So you'll notice you're feeling a bit hungry?

B   Yes – I have actually tried – you know, cooked a bit of fish and prepared something like that to eat and haven't been able to. I've tried that.

T   So you are very good at trying things out and testing where you are. You're not afraid of experimenting.

B   But I don't eat it and eventually throw it all away, but I have tried.

T   So you'd be beginning to develop an appetite. What else might you notice?

B   I don't, I know I wouldn't feel. Since I've been back two days I haven't vomited and I haven't used any laxatives and I feel quite good about that.

Miss Bonchance then says she hears two voices which sound real. While the therapist was wondering how seriously to take this the session goes into drift and the team suggests a short break. The decision to keep the parents out of the solution is reviewed and upheld and Miss Bonchance's 'customer' status is confirmed. She has also let the therapist know she must return to France after four weeks (though she is actually recalled after two). The sense of urgency and Miss Bonchance's own positive outlook lead the team to press for even more 'change talk'. They also decide not to take a 'psychiatric' view of the voices. The break is used to give Miss Bonchance some feedback on her successful handling of the problem so far and on the team's confidence that a solution will be forthcoming. Having highlighted those achievements which define her as a strong-willed, independent and adventurous person, the therapist asks Miss Bonchance about other situations in which she has had to struggle but has been successful in reaching her goal.

B   When I wanted to leave home. I think that is really it. I think that was the only time I really wanted to do something and wasn't allowed to do it.

T   What, leaving home?

B   So I just had to convince them – leaving school as well.

Miss Bonchance then describes how at first she tried to follow her mother's wishes by staying on at school and then decided for herself by getting a job.

T   Terrific – so you must be quite proud of yourself?

B   Yes, I am quite proud of myself. I did the same thing when I wanted to leave home – I found a job in France – it's a main office here and they've got an office there.

T   It's very clever because I guess your mother had mixed feelings. I guess she liked the idea of you being in France.

B   Yes I knew – I knew – because the office is very close to my father's town – it took about six months to find a job.

T   That's terrific – so it's a way to leave home while being loyal to your parents.

B   That's right.

T   Beautiful – they must have not known what to do.

B   I don't know (laughs). I bought the ticket before I found the job.

T   So – when you decide on something that's difficult you have some pretty imaginative ways to do it. Ways which are – which combine the apparently impossible – abandoning your parents and still being loyal to them. It's a beautiful way to do it. That's marvellous. I love that. I'd like to use that in my teaching if I might.

B   Yes (laughing).

Miss Bonchance is not untypical of someone developing a solution frame. In the early part of the session the frame is barely acknowledged but each time it fits – introduces 'news of a difference' to her own account – it leads to a further opening of strengths. The summary of her

...LUTION

...t yogurt this morning.

...eat yogurt – I found some fruit in it which made me heave –

...n't do anything.

...t that be the next stage – that you could eat yogurt with tiny

...fruit in it?

...e – it was tiny.

...ned potato – would that be something?

...l I'm not well informed because I thought potato was really

...ttening but I read something the other day which said peanuts

...ere eight times more fattening. I didn't know things like that. So to

...me I won't touch potato, bread, chocolate – anything like that.

Something says 'no'.

And when things are going OK do you eat things like this?

Not since this started. When I first went on a diet I'd eat one meal a

day but no bread or potatoes.

T   OK. So when things are OK what would you like to be eating?

B   I'd like to eat fish, meat – just what I'd eat before.

T   Would that include bread and potato or not?

B   Hopefully – hopefully I'd be at a stage – I'd worry about it if I ate
    normally and started to put on weight, I don't know what would
    happen then.

T   Is that thinking about it from where you are now or is that how you
    think you'll think when things are back to normal?

B   I was thinking about – even now, if I started to eat more and then saw
    I was putting on weight I don't know what would happen.

T   Well, one of the things from what you've said, I suppose you'll have
    these two voices going and one of them will say, 'Well done, you've
    put on a bit of weight, that's terrific – you're on the way forward' and
    the other voice would be saying 'Oh for God's sake what are you
    doing? You've put on weight, this is terrible!'

B   Yes.

T   So you'd have those two – sometimes one will be louder. Like when
    you'd done your O-levels your parents' voice was louder.

B   Yes, that's right.

T   And you went back to school and then your voice came louder and
    you saw your way through, so I guess there'd be that struggle and
    that's what we're looking for – I guess you're going to create an
    imaginative solution.

B   Yes.

strengths afforded by the break are readily accepted by Miss Bonchance and thus promote this enthusiastic account of her leaving home. For the first time she does not drop back into problem talk and for the next ten minutes, until the break, the talk is almost entirely problem-free and the solution, to both the team and Miss Bonchance, becomes an almost inevitable part of the future. These last ten minutes are also used to make a final decision on the route to solution and whether it needs to include the parents and whether the voices should be regarded as a problem. And as is often the case, at the last minute – literally – a hidden 'jewel' is revealed – the exception which begins the new rule.

The session continues:

T   So it's the sort of thing which can happen to anyone. It's just bad
    luck that it's taken this particular form.

B   Yes.

T   But you're the sort of person who does something about things so
    you're obviously going to stop it becoming -

B   Yes.

T   So it's not such a great problem. I'm interested that your parents
    came with you. Whose idea was that?

B   Not mine – my mother's.

T   So it was your mother's, but she didn't mind waiting down there?

B   She said she was going to come in but I said 'you're not.' I think she
    still thinks I'm my sister's age.

T   How old is your sister?

B   Seventeen, I think – so I said 'no, I'll be better on my own.'

T   You're very good at working compromises, aren't you?

B   Yes.

T   Which is nice and interesting because how you describe eating at the
    moment is in a similar way – a sort of conflict.

B   Yes.

T   Two different voices – your parents saying 'Go to school' and you
    saying 'Go to work' – and you describe that in the same way?

B   Yes.

T   Which I guess I would have a lot of confidence that you're going to
    find a constructive and imaginative way of appeasing both voices and
    getting on with your life.

B   I hope so.

T   Because if you can do it over leaving home – which some people say
    is the most difficult thing in the world to do in our society, to make
    that break – then you know I guess you'll be looking back on this as a

difficult time but one you found a nice solution to.

B   Yes.

T   (Pause) Um, you're going back to France towards the end of next month?

B   I don't know. I've got some more leave to come so maybe they'll be nice to me and let me stay until Christmas.

T   But it gives – um – it means if you want to go back to France with this difficulty behind you, you want to move fairly quickly on it.

B   Yes.

T   Now, we're generally – though we like to do things as quickly as possible – generally we like to move cautiously. But there's something about you which is quite a fast mover and a doer.

B   Yes.

T   Would you be prepared to take the risk of moving quickly on this or would you want us to be cautious and move a bit slower?

B   No, it's something that I've decided I've got to do – so I don't know.

T   Would you support our view that it's something we should be able to do something about to sort out?

B   Yes, I think so, it's something I've tried on my own. I think I've got past the stage by not vomiting or anything else.

T   Absolutely – which is the other thing I meant to say which is that if somebody comes here with a difficulty – a complaint – and then we find that they've already started to solve it before they get here then usually that means it's going to be solved pretty quickly because it's already en route.

B   Yes. I understand that because I'm sure that if I was back in my flat on my own I'd be carrying on.

T   Carrying on?

B   Carrying on the vomiting.

T   You do?

B   Yes.

T   What would have to be different then to stop you carrying on in your own flat other than taking your parents with you which wouldn't – or would that – be nice? Would you like to take them with you?

B   To the flat next door!

T   Would you like that?

B   Yes, I think so – or maybe it should be me coming back. But then again I couldn't live with them. I couldn't. I couldn't live with them for more than two or three weeks.

T   I think that's pretty healthy. I think m[...]

B   Yes it's normal – I'm sure it is. But I [...] able not to think where this is go[...] on my way.

T   So if you move things forward he[...] France they might slip back a little [...] little bit and you'll be able to move th[...]

B   I think, I mean I don't really want to co[...] don't mind for two or three months but yo[...] everything sorted out here and then when I t[...] back I will.

T   Is there anything you think your parents can contr[...] this forward quickly or is it something you think you[...] yourself?

B   I think I've got to do it by myself.

T   Right.

B   They're very good about it – they're not throwing food at me.

T   So they trust you?

B   Yes, I asked them not to do that because it has happened to me in the past when I've had 'You've got to eat this, you've got to eat that.' You seem to retaliate. You can't say no when you've got to that stage.

T   So they trust you enough to know you'll look after yourself?

The therapist's statement is designed to select out that aspect of Miss Bonchance's relationship with her parents most likely to support her own view of recovery. She has explicitly referred to relationship difficulties and also implied a connection between these and the eating problems. Any improvement in this area is therefore likely to aid the solution process. Many therapeutic approaches would suggest more attention to this issue, particularly as the parents have been associated with the onset of the problem and with the initial improvements (by their twenty-four hour surveillance). However, were this 'problem' to be identified by the therapist he would still be seeing evidence of the client's solution and amplifying it. In other words, the statement: 'So they trust you enough…' would still be made. Solution talk does not require problem specificity!

Miss Bonchance replies affirmatively:

B   Yes. I've told them – I can eat soups, ice cream, anything soft I don't have to chew on. And that's what is done.

T   What would be the next stage of food if you were making a transition between very soft food and…

T   What I'm trying to find out is the voice which is saying, 'I don't want this problem any more.' What will that voice be saying? What will it be pleased about?

B   An example – yesterday I felt absolutely great and I even had some bread in my soup. I even did that.

T   And you ate some?

B   I really mushed it up.

T   So you actually had some bread?

B   I'd done something about it. I'd gone out and I'd done something. I came home and said to my Dad I'd have some bread.

T   Fantastic.

B   And then today I got up OK, I had a coffee for breakfast and then I had the soup and I felt really bloated, I felt -

T   Sure. That's the other side of it, isn't it? But there's this other side which is saying 'Great – you did it – you actually had some BREAD!'

B   Yes. But I felt awful about it today and I was thinking there's only one bowl of soup and usually I'm not hungry. Then I thought, oh yes, I had some bread yesterday.

T   So you are actually on the move already, not only about not vomiting but also about eating solid food?

B   Yes. It had to be mushed up and he'd left the sides on the bread and I couldn't -

T   Good.

As the therapist interrupts Miss Bonchance in order to punctuate and endorse the 'solution' aspect of this statement, he in turn is interrupted by the team suggesting it is time for the break.

T   Where was I?

B   I'd put some bread in my soup!

T   Yes! So presumably what you're saying is that you want this out of the way, there's only one voice you need to listen to.

B   Yes.

T   And there's one voice you need to find ways not to listen to.

B   Yes, that's right.

T   And to discount or not hear the same as in the end you had for a period to discount or not hear your parents' voice and allow your own voice to come through is one of the things which must be happening for you to be doing what you are already doing. You must be finding ways to put one voice to one side or to take less notice of it and you're beginning to hear the other voice louder and that is something we need to think about. I'm going to have my break now and I'll be about 5 or 10 minutes.

And so Miss Bonchance's view that this is a problem for herself to sort out is firmly established; the voices, potentially an escalation of the problem, are incorporated into the solution and we have found Miss Bonchance has already started to eat solids.

The discussion in the break is almost exactly reported in the feedback to Miss Bonchance and the task is derived from a case of marital therapy reported in *Clues* (de Shazer, 1988). In this instance the therapist took notes of the discussion and took them back into the room with Miss Bonchance. The compliments and task take about five minutes, sometimes delivered haltingly with a search for the right words and sometimes with fluency. A very strong rapport has grown between the therapist and Miss Bonchance and while the therapist talks she constantly nods and speaks her assent. Both are enjoying themselves.

The feedback and task are reported in full:

T   We've got some ideas – and I've just thought of another one. I write these things down or I forget them all. Right, we've taken you at your word which is to go the 'fast way'.

B   Uhmm.

T   Which seems like – we wouldn't have been persuaded to do that if it hadn't been the various qualities you've shown like your strong-mindedness, the quick identification of the problem and the clarity with which you can think about it and work on it. We very much liked the way you broke it down into these two voices because we actually know what to do now.

B   Yes.

T   We know which voice to listen to. And the fact that, yes, you're more than halfway to solving it before you got here – which is very nice for us – and for you too, because I guess even without coming here you might well have solved it anyway because you are certainly on the right track.

B   Yes.

T   It does, you do certainly seem more than half way to solving it and the thing I particularly like, because it's the sort of thing I like, is the complete individuality of your solution-finding and the thing I'm going to look forward to most is hearing what it was in this case.

B   Yes.

T   Because I think it's going to be as creative as getting a job near your father's village.

B   Right. *(laughing)*

T   But look, we've got – we'd like to offer you an appointment next week. Could you do the same time next week?

B   Yes.

T   Good, because we don't want to leave it too long because of the time. But if you were around longer we would have left it longer. Yes, because when someone is doing as well as you are we don't want to interfere too much.

B   Right.

T   Because we might set it back but as there is this speed thing we'll have to do things more quickly. So I want to give you something to do which is quite a lot at the end of a first session. We might give it at the end of a second or third session but I think it will be something well within your capacities.

B   Right.

T   What made me think of it was something you said – you saying that before you went to sleep at night you thought about the next day and wondered what it was going to be like. Now, again, that's a very good thing to be doing and what we often suggest to people is that they do just that so we'd like to capitalise on that. What we'd like you to do is actually make a decision about the next day – whether the next day is a day on which you are going to do something about getting out of the difficulty or not.

B   Yes.

T   But we'd like you to make that decision by tossing a coin and deciding if the next day is a day on which you are going to do something about it or not. So each night, between now and when we next meet, toss a coin to decide whether the next day is a day you are going to do something about it or not. And if you want you can do best out of three or best out of five or whatever you like.

B   Yes.

T   So if it's your decision to do something about it, you've already said a number of things you do when the problem is less, like you go for a walk, window shopping, getting a video to look at, eating something different, contacting a friend. Now those, one, two, three, four, five things – and maybe when you think about it there'll be more – I'm sure there are! What we'd like you to do is, when you've tossed the coin and decided the next day will be a day you're going to do something, choose the easiest, the thing you think which on the next day will be easiest. And that will vary, of course, depending on your mood. What you feel like one day, the next you might think,

'Well hell, I've watched enough videos' – but make it the easiest and do that. And notice what happens. The other thing I'd like you to do between now and next week is notice the things your parents do or say that help – and report back.

So it's tossing a coin, picking the easiest of the routes to solving the problem and, just by the by, notice what your parents do that helps. OK?

B   Yes, OK.

T   And I'll see you in a week.

B   Thanks. Thank you. I actually feel better now, that was very helpful.

Though drawn directly from de Shazer the task almost entirely employs behaviour Miss Bonchance is already doing – it also uses her language. The coin is a typical example of the de Shazer team's creativity. Because good days in Miss Bonchance's life are unpredictable and therefore depend on chance, an element of the randomness needs to be included in the task. The coin provides this.

The Second Session

de Shazer emphasizes the value of starting the next session positively. 'How have things been?' is usually taken as an invitation to 'talk problems' and we have learned to avoid this where possible.

The first minute or so of the second session went:

T   So how did your – I set you a rather difficult task?

B   I had a really busy week.

T   Did you – what have you been doing?

B   Everything. I've been going out, I've seen all my friends, I took Mum and Dad to the cinema last night. I've been at home a little bit in the mornings mainly but then I've just been out. I planned it all a day ahead.

T   Good heavens! So tell me about how you managed the tossing of the coin and things.

B   That was all right. I just decided. And every day has been good. I'm feeling really positive. The only thing is that my office phoned this morning and I've got to go back next week.

T   Next week! What do you think about that?

B   I don't mind because they've given me the time at Christmas, so – that's the only thing – but I wasn't expecting that. I've planned everything the day before. I've sat down before the day ended and thought, like, I'll go out with my Mum tomorrow, I'll go shopping.

T   So you gave up tossing the coin and decided you were going to do things anyway.

B   No, I tossed the coin and eventually ended up playing heads and tails with my sister *(laughing)*.

T   Did you!!

B   Yes and it did help because I had that in my mind – I had to do it – so by doing that I had to decide what I was going to do the next day.

T   Good heavens! So the night before you decided what you were going to do. Because last week I thought I was moving fast when I was asking you to do the easiest of a list of things and you've gone and done them all and a lot more.

The session goes from strength to strength but it is still some considerable time before Miss Bonchance reveals the extent of her success – the fact that she had been eating normally for two days. Because she was going out each day, her parents had gone back to work. Miss Bonchance took pity on them having to work while she was on holiday, so cooked for them. After two days of this she thought it was silly not to eat with them, so she cooked food for everyone, had a complete meal, felt a bit sick but decided that was only to be expected and had no intention of allowing herself to 'slip into that state again'. She had heard nothing from her voices but she had received a call from her boss asking her to return to work because of a crisis. She then raised a new problem, her anxiety about going into crowded places on her own. We eventually discovered that she never needed to go to such places on her own, always being able to arrange to go with others. This seemed a good enough solution to both Miss Bonchance and the therapist. But another problem was raised – panic attacks in social situations which sometimes led her to decline invitations. Indeed she was just considering turning down an invitation to dinner. We discovered that often she was lively and sociable at parties and that the panics were unpredictable. She was able to list a variety of social skills she could use when not in a panic and some she used when she felt a panic attack coming on. We then considered the invitation in the light of these 'facts' and in the context of her creative problem-solving. So when asked what she would do, the answer was a forgone conclusion: 'I'll toss my coin!' she said.

    The ease with which Miss Bonchance was able to apply her newly-discovered solution skills to these additional problems suggested they had been well incorporated into her everyday repertoire and were not simply the preserve of therapy or the eating difficulty. Miss Bonchance did not expect a relapse. Not that she thought the problem had gone for good but rather she was confident that she would not allow it to develop far as it had on this occasion. And if it did? She would follow the same solution pattern – come home and call the therapist!

CHAPTER SEVEN

FAISAL'S LAST CHANCE:
WORK WITH ADOLESCENTS IN A SCHOOL CONTEXT

This chapter will describe a solution focused brief thrapy project that has been undertaken in a state comprehensive mixed secondary school of some 850 pupils (ages 11 to 18) in inner London. The project, begun in September 1997, is still ongoing.

THE PROJECT

The idea for a project came from the school itself. Members of staff had attended training courses offered by the Brief Therapy Practice and were keen to see solution focused therapy used more consistently in the school. They approached the Practice with a view to a therapist coming into the school to counsel, one to one, young people (generally aged between 12 and 16) who were seen as having behavioural problems and who, in many cases, had had to be excluded in the past. They were very concerned to try to prevent permanent exclusion of these pupils.

The project began with a 15-week pilot of weekly morning sessions, spread over the first two terms of the school year, 1997-8. As the feeling grew that it was proving effective, so it was agreed to extend the project by a further 10 weeks to the end of the summer term. Following this, the Practice was invited to continue the project into a second year.

THE YOUNG PEOPLE

The therapist is known in the school as the 'brief therapist'. The young people referred are given the choice as to whether they wish to attend or not. Comments occasionally made to the therapist make it clear that for many the therapy is regarded as a punishment for bad behaviour and this has led him to regard this client group as largely 'reluctant'. Sometimes a student asks whether something they are talking about can be regarded as confidential. The therapist makes it clear that confidentiality ends when he regards something he is hearing as being of concern from a safety point of view, and there have been a few occasions when he has had to let the student know he will be sharing information with staff. Parental permission has been obtained in advance of the student being seen, as the therapist is not a member of the school staff.

PRACTICAL ISSUES

A room is booked for the sessions – a large room usually used for meetings (the therapist has, on occasion, found that that is exactly what the room is being used for when he has arrived to see his first client of the morning!). The therapist is given minimal information regarding the client in advance of seeing them, and in some cases he has had no information at all. This has been perfectly satisfactory, since from a solution focused point of view it is not necessary for the therapist to enquire about the problem – only that the student and/or the school have a hope for things to be different in his or her life. The therapist has requested that before each *follow-up* session with a client he is given the latest information on what is known about changes since the previous session, and when this is possible it is provided in hand-written form. There is almost no time available for staff to meet with the therapist, except for some hurried conversations in the staff room. On one or two occasions it has been important for the therapist to join a meeting of staff with a student he has been seeing, sometimes with a parent present as well.

Originally it was arranged that a young person would be 'booked in' for a counselling session that would last the length of a lesson, i.e. fifty minutes. In practice, by the time a student arrives and the session begins, there is rarely more than forty or forty-five minutes available. However, the length of sessions has got progressively shorter as more and more students have been squeezed into the slots available. The therapist has, in fact, welcomed this development, as he experiments with the limits of 'brief' therapy. Most first sessions are now completed in thirty minutes, and follow-up sessions require only ten to fifteen minutes.

FAISAL'S LAST CHANCE

We will now look at a case in detail, with the transcripts of the two sessions that took place being reproduced almost in their entirety, except for some minor adjustments to safeguard the young person's confidentiality. The two sessions lasted 34 and 23 minutes respectively. The therapist knew nothing at all about the client at the start of the first session, other than his name.

First session

T   According to the note I've got, we're meeting until 11.30 – that gives us 25 minutes. I don't actually know very much about you at all. How do you spell your name?

F   'F-a-i-s-a-l.'

T   And you're how old?

F   13. I'm gonna be 14 in three weeks time.

T   What's your tutor's name?

F   Miss Jones.

T   Tell me a bit about yourself. What sort of person you are, what sort
    of things you like…

Here the therapist begins in the getting-to-know-you fashion we call
'problem free talk', emphasising that as much as possible the client is
encouraged to talk about themselves as a person and not as a problem
on two legs.

F   First I come from Eritrea, my country. My dad and my mum split up
    when I was very young and then I came here with my aunt. I lived
    with her and then I moved away from her because we didn't get
    along, so I moved in with my Nan, since then I lived there. Before I
    used to be interested in sport, I used to play for a lot of teams, but
    since then everything has changed. Before, I used to get in trouble
    with the Police and all that, I used to be worse than this, but I've
    calmed down now, now it's occurring again, now I'm getting in
    more trouble.

T   So, er, who do you live with at the moment?

F   My Nan.

T   Your Nan. So where are your mum and dad?

F   In Eritrea.

T   Do you have any brothers, sisters…
    I have one sister who used to go to this school, my cousins, they've
    finished school.

T   Are your mum and dad OK?

F   Yes.

T   Do you get to go back and see them at all?

F   No, they phone. I can go back, they phone sometimes and I speak to
    them, and send letters. I prefer to stay here, for my future. I've got
    everything planned out, in a way.

T   Have you? What sort of plans have you got? Tell me about that.

Solution focused therapy is, of course, characterised by an intense
interest on the part of the therapist in the client's preferred problem-
free future. Therefore as soon as Faisal refers to planning for his future,
the therapist takes that as the perfect opportunity to encourage such a
conversation. He would, if the conversation had gone differently, have

nted to learn a little bit more about Faisal. As it is, he has already
begun to see him as a resourceful young man who has experienced a
great deal in his short life: he is, unquestionably, a survivor who must
have learned to stand on his own two feet from an early age.

F   Hopefully, if I do well, if I calm down and do well, hopefully I'll go
to college and do something in art and design.

T   Art and design?

F   Before I used to do sports, but now I don't think I can do that,
because my body's changing and things like that.

T   Yes!

F   Before I used to be a lot faster but now a lot of things have changed
in my mind – looking for a job.

T   Do you have a Saturday job?

F   Before. A person who really knew me very well, knew I was good, so
he let me, behind the till. I got experience there. I was excluded
from my other school, and I didn't have school for nearly six
months and so I was working there, since I was excluded.

T   So how long have you been at this school?

F   Since January.

T   Only since January. *(The session is taking place in June)*

F   At first I had it in my mind to be good. But in the last few months
things start going bad.

T   Right so, what would you be hoping – do you mind me taking notes
while we're talking?

F   I don't mind.

T   An important question for me would be what would you be hoping
to get out of today's meeting. What would tell you this has been a
good meeting today?

F   Normally, if I'm telling what's wrong, why I'm normally angry or
something I just hold it down. If you hold it too much you have to
release it, that might have caused a fight or something like that.

T   So if you release your feelings… what happens if you're able to
release your feelings?

F   I talk about it more easier… normally, if someone gets me angry, I
just take it down and I hold it down and then if they do it again, I
get more mad, I'm a person with a short temper, I get mad quickly,
straight away.

T   I see. So if we talked about some of the things that are bothering
you, you would feel that would get it sort of out, and then what?

F   Then try and sort it out, possibly.

T   Yeah. And then you would feel what?

F   More confident about it. Normally I talk to my Nan, but there are some things you can't talk to my Nan that she don't agree with, so I don't talk to her that much.

T   Right. So you see this as something private that you can talk about here that you can't talk about elsewhere?

F   No, it's not that, I don't mind, it's all the same.

T   It's all the same, it's just *who* you can talk with…

F   Yeah.

T   So, you'd like to be able to talk about things *so that* you can feel more comfortable with yourself.

F   Yeah, and sort it out.

T   And then, if you're feeling you're more comfortable with yourself, what difference does this make to how things go in school, for example?

F   I'll have more, like, self-esteem, to do better and things like that, or…

T   What do you mean by 'self-esteem'?

It is very common for professionals involved with young people to hear them using language that they could only have picked up from adults. There is nothing 'wrong' with that – so long as they are encouraged to explain, in *their* words, what they mean!

F   I mean like I feel like have done something well, that I talked about it. Normally I just keep it in and I don't tell nobody about it and it makes things worse in the end and I take it out on somebody else. If I could talk about it, I feel more better. If I can't talk about it I just keep it in and I'd be more angrier, and my school work don't go that well as well.

T   It's not going that well at the moment?

F   No.

T   So you feel that when you came to the school it started off with good intentions to get on with the work and do things, and you feel it's sliding down now?

F   Yeah.

T   OK, is there a particular, er…

F   Reason?

T   Yeah, reason, problem, that you think you want me to hear about now?

As de Shazer has stated in his presentations, being solution-focused does not mean being 'problem-phobic'. As the therapist had no information about Faisal from staff, it seemed reasonable to check if there were any other concerns that he needed to know about. An alternative question would have been, 'What do you think your tutor [or head of year etc.] would be hoping to see different as a result of this meeting?'

F   Yeah, it's about smoking, probably.

T   Smoking?

F   Yeah, that's what annoys me the most. 'Cos before I used to be a very healthy person, I used to like go out playing football everyday, in my spare time. But now I've changed. That's making me more slower. And even my coach told me that if I carried on I wouldn't have no future in the team.

T   So what's it about smoking, I didn't quite follow what was the problem there?

F   I can't stop smoking, I'm smoking too much, it makes me worse.

T   Right.

F   Physically as well. I thought before that when people tell you smoking is bad for you I used to think they were just saying that, but now I found out it really does do something to you *(he coughs)*.

T   Like that cough *(laughs)*.

F   No, no, that's because I've got a cold.

T   *(laughs)*

F   Yeah, in a way it's like that!

T   So, there's that, smoking slows you down, and generally you said there are some changes in your body.

F   Yeah, I'm slower. Before I used to run 14 lengths of a full sized pitch in training, but now I haven't even done properly five. I start faster, then I get slower, I can't breathe properly…

The 'right' time to ask the 'miracle question' is when the therapist feels the client is engaged and there is a degree of co-operation in the therapist/client relationship towards change. In this particular session, the question could well have been asked five minutes earlier – for example, at Faisal's first mention of having plans.

T   So, let me just ask you a strange question for a moment. If a miracle was to happen tonight while you're asleep and the problems that have brought you here were solved, overnight, but you didn't know, because you were asleep when this miracle happened, what would be different tomorrow that would tell you that the problems that had brought you here were solved?

F   Everything. Smoking and everything.

T   OK. Tell me what would be different, what would be happening in your life instead?

F   I'd be more calm, and be more... interested in... like, school and my life.

T   So, if you were calm, what would you be like then, how would you handle situations, being calm?

F   That's a hard one, let me think of it.

T   Umm...

T   If I was more calm, if I knew what was happening... I'd think about the things I was doing, and things like that, what's happening there. Normally, I don't think, I just butt into the thing, I just go to one conclusion.

T   So how would you deal with things differently after a miracle's happened?

F   Probably more calm... and more... more thinking.

T   Calm and thinking about things and not just jumping to one conclusion?

F   Yeah.

T   Yeah. So if you were more interested in school, what sort of things would you be interested in?

F   Er... probably go to Art, or homework club, or things like that.

T   Yes. Art, homework club... yeah...

F   PE, do a training, try to get back into my team.

T   Right. And you said also you'd be more interested in life. What would be a sign the miracle had happened and you'd be more interested in *life*?

F   Er, the way I'm going it looks like I want to grow up too fast. I shouldn't. I'm thinking about work and all that stuff, and I shouldn't at my age.

T   Right, so you might relax about some of those things. So what would you be interested in instead then?

F   Be a calm person. Have an eye on my work and everything like that.

T   You mean, school work?

F   Yeah.

T   So, you'd think about your school work?

F   Yeah. Before I wasn't interested, but now I'm trying to improve. Since I got excluded two weeks ago I haven't got into trouble like I have become... because I was on report, but I've been good since then.

As happens in most cases, the client spontaneously introduces an 'exception' – a recent small sign that the miracle is already starting to happen. The therapist's best response here should be to acknowledge the recent success and 'log it' for future reference, but return to the miracle narrative as soon as possible in order to maintain the intensity of its telling.

T   So you've been on report two weeks…

F   No, I've only been on report for one week, but I've been good two weeks.

T   So you've been calmer in the last two weeks.

F   Sometimes I think of what I'm doing, I know I'm doing something bad, but I say to myself, why aren't you stopping.

T   What? Sorry… ?

F   One time I said to myself, why are you messing around in the class. I was watching this boy doing his work. He's only doing his work I said to myself, how come you're not doing that, you're not interested in your work like him.

T   OK. Just going back to the miracle. How would your Nan know a miracle's happened, without you having to tell her?

F   Happier. Do my homework. Come home earlier from school.

T   *(writing)* 'Earlier from school' – what sort of time is that?

F   About five… no, five is late. About four. Something like that. And the next thing for school would be being prepared for school.

T   How would your Nan know you were prepared for school?

F   Because in the morning it's a big rush for me. I have to pack up my books and everything like that.

T   So you'd be more prepared.

F   Yeah.

T   So she would see you organising things… what, the night before, or in the morning?

F   No, night before. When I wake up, everything's ready.

T   OK. Do you think she'd be pleased to see these things?

It is usually very helpful to encourage clients to reflect on the response of significant others to the miracle happening, and to expand on the client's feelings and responses to others' responses! Not all solution focused therapists think it is so important to be quite so detailed in the description of the after-miracle scenario, but as this sequence shows, detailed questioning can yield up elements of difference that may be important to the client in future.

F   Yeah.

T   How would you know?

F   Because once I have been good and she tells me I've been good and I should be good and all that stuff. I don't tell her when I'm being bad, 'cos when I'm good she gives me more time to do more things and to enjoy myself.

T   Right.

F   Or – and when I'm bad, I have to do chores, and things like that, and stay in the house.

T   Right. So, when she's pleased with you what will you see? Say if you come home before five o'clock…

F   She'll tell me how I'm early, and how I've been good, and everything like that.

T   And then when you talk to her, she'll be pleased, and you'll know that because she will…?

F   She'll tell me that and she'll do things for me.

T   She'll do things for you…? Like what?

F   She might give me money. She gives me money, but she might give me money to go places.

T   Right. It sounds like you would enjoy that, if she was happy with you and helping you, you'd be pleased about that?

F   Hmm.

T   That will make things nicer at home?

F   Yes. At home things aren't *bad*. I just come in, watch TV, do homework, go to school. On weekends I don't stay in much.

T   So after the miracle you'd be expected to spend a bit more time at home?

F   No! I really don't want to spend much time at home. I want to be out with my friends.

T   Sure. So what would she see different?

F   Normally, I don't ask my Nan if I can go out – I just sneak out and then I just come back. I should ask her and then she might let me 'cos she'll say 'you've been good, you can go out'.

T   Right. So you'll be telling her about going out, you'll be communicating a bit more?

F   Yeah.

T   So that would be different?

F   Yeah.

T   *(checks watch)* I'm worried about time. Who would be the first teacher, first member of staff in the school who would notice that something's different, that the miracle's happened?

F   There's a lot of teachers. My tutor…

T   What would she see that would tell her a miracle's happened?

F   If I wore my uniform more often and came into school more, and be more calm in registration and not running out and coming in.

T   *(writing)* 'Calmer in registration'. What else?

F   In lessons, I'd be good, and not join in people's arguments and things like that.

T   In lessons, not joining in arguments…

F   Carry on doing my work.

T   *(writing)* 'Carry on my work'.

F   And there's one teacher, Miss Calvert…

T   How would she know?

F   'Cos normally, when I'm bad, I'm sent to her office, every week I'm there.

T   So she'd know 'cos she wouldn't be seeing so much of you!

F   Yeah. She'd probably hear good things about me. Teachers think I'm really bad, but I'm not. When I do my work in a lesson, they're like, really surprised, like 'you've been good' and they tell other teachers and things like that.

T   So they express surprise, and you're thinking, 'but this is me!'

F   Yeah, normal me.

T   So they would see you not joining in arguments, carrying on with your work…

F   …not chatting that much.

T   Not chatting much. Is there a particular friend you've made since coming to this school?

F   I've made enough. I knew people from this school before.

T   OK, so you knew people before. So, who's like your best friend?

F   I've got a lot of friends.

T   Just name one.

F   There's a boy called Mohammed. I was with him yesterday when we had the fight.

T   Oh, the fight. I heard about this fight.

Inevitably, when working in an institution, a therapist will hear clients refer to issues that involve other clients they see. In this case, the therapist had already seen a young man called Darren earlier that morning who had described his involvement in a fight. He hadn't mentioned Faisal by name.

F   Yeah. I was with him. He lives next to my house. We go everywhere, play football together, do everything together – that's the closest person that knows me.

T   Did you get involved with this fight? I understand it was between him and another boy, Darren.

F   Yeah, I helped him. I didn't actually hit nobody, but I said to myself 'don't' because I knew I was going to be excluded so you might as well sort this out sensibly. He had a fight and the other person – I was just watching – the other person was going to join in, so we stopped it.

T   You mean, Dwight?

This, again, was knowledge the therapist had gained from seeing Darren earlier.

F   Yeah.

T   So how did you stop yourself getting involved with it and just left it to Mohammed?

F   No, at first I told him there's no point fighting, 'cos me and him we're the same, we've got our last chance. We agreed together that we won't get into trouble.

T   You agreed that between you and Mohammed?

F   Yeah.

T   Great, great! But there *was* trouble yesterday – how did you keep out of it?

F   Me, I… I… er… I, I didn't start cursing back or anything like that.

T   Right. Great!

F   I never made myself noticeable like. I stayed quiet.

T   Right.

F   I stopped it, 'cos…

T   *You* stopped it?

F   Yeah, the fight. If I was gonna say, 'What are you looking at my friend for', and all that, that means I'm in trouble, but if I stop it that means I'm not joining nobody's side…

T   How did you stop it?

F   It started out they were pushing each other. First my friend was gonna hit him, and I warned him, 'Don't do this! Don't do this! The teachers are standing there, the boys, all this', so we went round the corner, and he ran, I saw my friend running, because the boy went like this to him *(stabs his finger into his chest)*, Darren…

T   I'm just interested in what you actually did…

F   I took them apart *(demonstrates pulling two people apart)*. I took my friend away and I told him to calm down, and Dwight was going to punch my friend when he was putting his shoes on and I holded Dwight…

Right, so you tried to calm things down…

Yeah.

T   OK. Supporting your friend Mohammed, you two have an agreement between you not to get into trouble.

F   Yeah.

T   Right. That's terribly important. Let me ask you another strange question, and moving a little bit quickly with some of this because I know we haven't got much time.

The same comment made earlier regarding the timing of introducing the 'miracle question' applies to the use of 'scale questions'. In this instance the therapist feels that a) he has a fair description of Faisal's preferred future, and b) the 'exception' in relation to yesterday's fight sounds very important indeed, so a rating scale seems appropriate.

T   If I take, like, a sort of 0 to 10 scale (draws on note pad). If I said 10 is the miracle's happened, all the things you've told me about that you want to see different, your interest in school and life, you're calmer, OK, and your Nan's seeing changes and she's rewarding you for that, Miss Calvert is hearing good things and you're not getting into fights and trouble, you're not chatting too much in class and so on; that's a 10. But 0 is, well…

F   Just the same?

T   …chucked out I suppose, 0 is the absolute worst thing, they can't stand any more and you've got to leave. So, 10 is the miracle, and 0 is sort of out of school. Where would you say things are at, now, today, between 0 and 10?

F   Around 8.

T   8!!!! Wow! Gosh! OK. So you see it as 8 today. What tells you it's that high?

The therapist is, of course, taken aback at how high Faisal has estimated things. He is unable to contain his disbelief, which is not at all helpful! So he tries to get back to an accepting stance by saying 'OK'. It's not important for the therapist either to believe or disbelieve the client, but simply to encourage clients to explain *their* view. A not-knowing stance, combined with a respectful curiosity, is essential for effective therapy. It doesn't matter a great deal if Faisal says 0.8, 8 or 80 – as long as he is above 0, there is the potential to find and develop exceptions.

F   Yesterday it was about 9, or 10 actually.

T   Was it?

F   Yeah, 'cos I surprised myself. I didn't join in. Normally I would. I don't like it when people want to fight my friends. I would join in, I would have done more worse.

T   So yesterday was *really* different for you.

F   Yeah.

T   That was sort of, like a miracle day, because you didn't get involved in the fight.

F   Yeah.

T   Fantastic!

F   Yeah. I just stopped it. Even though they were supposed to be my enemies, I told them to break it up. And other people shouted out, 'hit him!' and 'hit him!' and 'hit him!'

T   So, there was… yes I heard there was a lot of people starting to gather.

F   Yeah.

T   So you were really pleased with yourself yesterday; you feel good about what you did yesterday?

F   Yeah.

T   So yesterday was a real sign of how it can be?

F   Yeah.

T   OK. What else… you said you'd been on report the last two weeks and you've been a lot calmer. Tell me a bit about what tells you you've reached an 8 today.

F   Uniform, white shirt, come in early to registration this morning. I woke up early, packed up my stuff and left early.

T   Really? How did you manage that this morning?

F   My Nan woke me up, normally I just sit down and watch TV and when my friend comes I tell him to come down and watch TV with me and we're normally late, but today I got ready, and he normally comes for me but today I went for him and knocked for him.

T   Umm. Great. So this morning was brilliant, you've really worked hard at it to make it go well this morning.

F   Yeah.

T   And you say you're at 8 now. Are you on track for this being a really super day, do you think?

F   Yeah.

T   A miracle type day?

F   Yeah, if I don't tell people about the fight, it will. I could be at 10, but I started telling my friends about the fight and that's made it 8.

The focus now switches to what the signs would be of Faisal moving further up the scale. Typical questions at this point could be, 'What will ɔe different that will tell you you've reached 9?' or 'Let's say at the end of today you realise it's a 9, what will you be telling yourself you did to get there?'

T   Right. So, if you don't talk about the fight for the rest of the day, it'll make it a better day.

F   Yeah.

T   How will you stop yourself talking about it?

F   Just don't tell nobody. 'Cos there are people that, we call them 'two-faced', they act like your friend, they say, 'Oh, did you beat him up?' and when you tell them something they run back to the other person and tell them.

T   That's right.

F   I hate people like that. That's what annoys me.

T   So how do you stop yourself? If somebody says something to you and you say, 'No, that's not what happened', how are you gonna stop yourself getting involved?

F   I won't even speak about it.

T   How are you gonna stop yourself?

F   I would just say, 'Just forget about it, it was then, this is now.'

T   Yeah.

F   I would just tell them, 'I don't want to get in trouble.' Normally if somebody asks me questions like that, I'll just tell them, 'Why are you starting trouble for?', because people that ask me about the fight, they're the ones that want to start trouble.

T   Yeah, so you're confident that you can keep your lips sealed today?

F   Yeah.

T   Do you reckon you can do it?

F   Yeah.

T   And… but we're gonna have to stop in a moment, would you like to meet again so that we can follow up on how things are going?

F   Yeah.

T   OK. We've talked about today. What do you think over the next week will be important for you to be doing to help move towards 10 on the scale?

F   I had an essay to do but I didn't do it. Probably do that essay. A few homeworks.

T   Umm.

F   Ask my Nan if I can go out.

T   Ask your Nan.

F   She'll let me, but I just can't be bothered.

T   So, if you talk to her she'll be pleased, will she?

F   Yeah. She don't mind if I don't ask her, it's just better to tell her, to talk more, communicate more.

T   Right.

F   Come in early; cut down how much I'm smoking.

T   *(writing)* 'Cut down smoking'. We haven't talked much about that, you did mention that earlier. What would be a sign to you that you were cutting down on your smoking?

F   Er, if I never had more craving for cigarettes.

T   Oh, that would be a miracle, not to have cravings! *(laughs)*.

This is the dream for anyone with a so-called addiction problem – not just a cessation of the behaviour, but also an eradication of the cravings! The therapist decides not to accept that as a realistic goal – and certainly not as only a sign of progress.

The ensuing sequence, although in this instance related to the relatively minor issue of a young man reducing his cigarette smoking, is indicative of the Solution Focused approach to all addiction problems:

1) Whatever the client's behavioural goal, *whether abstinence or controlled use,* is accepted as valid. (Faisal is unclear whether he wants to stop altogether or not; but he is clear he wants to cut down). The element of choice – and therefore of control – is paramount.

2) Change can be a process of *small steps,* of gradual reduction (e.g. three rather than five cigarettes), if that is appropriate to the client.

3) The therapist will focus on what the client will *do* instead of using (e.g. be with different people).

4) Since feelings such as cravings will be expected to continue, at least for a time, the therapist will need to explore the client's preferred ways of *coping* with those feelings (e.g. do sport).

F   Oh, cut down how much I smoke – the times I have. Like today, already, before I came to school, I had four.

T   You've already had four this morning?

F   On the way to school me and my friend smoked together.

T   So, what would be a sign to you today that you were cutting back on your smoking?

F   If I didn't smoke none now, 'cos four is bad for a whole day.

T   So if you could keep off smoking today…

F   Or just probably one when I get home, 'cos I know I'm gonna need it.

T   If you had five a day for the moment would that be better than what you're usually having at the moment?

F   Usually if I have three, it's alright. With my friend... for me, just one and a half would be all right.

T   How are you gonna do that? How are you gonna cut back? 'Cos you're gonna have the cravings, I know that, they'll carry on for a while...

F   I notice that if I do more sport, it helps in a way, it makes you more healthier and everything. Probably try to do more sport.

T   More sport.

F   Yeah. Normally I smoke when someone annoys me, it calms me down.

T   So today, if people are winding you up about the fight, you're trying not to talk about it, you're gonna want to have a cigarette?

F   Yeah, in a way.

T   So what will you do instead of having a cigarette today? What will be your way of dealing with it?

F   I'll just move away from all this chaos.

T   Move away from it.

F   'Cos there are a lot of people who have said to me they want me to do good. Not just the teachers, my friends. There are a few girls in year 10 who are my close friends and they told me to stop smoking, they said it's gonna kill you and all this and be good. 'Cos they want me to get a good future, and I know what they mean. So if I hang around with them more, 'cos they speak sense, and I know that and normally I just hang around with the boys and they're always up to no good!

T   So, being with different people?

F   Yeah.

T   Is that gonna be easy for you to do?

F   Yeah. Since I got excluded I've been hanging around with them and my friend Mohammed. They've helped me. I've calmed down.

T   Good.

The session has to end – time is up – and the therapist wants to finish with constructive feedback for the client. Ideally, the therapist will take a formal break, leaving the room to think about what feedback to give and then returning to offer it. This is easy in clinical situations and home visits, but less so in a place like a school, with its environmental and time limitations. The therapist chooses to quickly scan his notes and deliver feedback on the hoof, so to speak. The repetition of 'Yeah' from the client implies Faisal is in agreement with the message and therefore it acts as a further spur to action. Unusually, the therapist decided not to add a suggestion of something the client could look out for in future.

T   OK. Look, we're supposed to finish now. Let me just say something about what I've learned about you today, because I've made quite a lot of notes here, even in a short time. I'm really impressed with how you've come here today, you've not met me before. You're very honest and open about things. You're telling me things aren't going as well as they could be at the moment. ('Yeah'). You've been very prepared to talk about things and how difficult things have been but also to work hard to think about how things *should be* in the future. ('Yeah'). And you've been able to look with me at all the different areas of your life at school, at home, friends, everything and your smoking, to think about how things should be different. What's really impressive is that it's not pie in the sky. You're saying to me, 'This is possible for me, ('Yeah'), I've really made an improvement in the last two weeks. I've been calmer in the last two weeks and yesterday I did something I was really impressed with by staying out of the fight and not only staying out of it, I tried to calm it down.' And all the ideas you've got *(turning pages of notepad)* for moving on and making sure next week will be a good week for you. You're confident you can do it and I must say listening to you and talking to you I can feel confident that you *will* see more changes over the next week, you will be trying to deal with your smoking, you will be trying to be with different people.

F   Normally I just say to myself, 'Forget about it, you're gonna stop next week...'

T   Yeah, but now you're really trying to deal with it, not putting if off.

F   ...now it's the point, it's in my face.

T   Yeah, now's the time to really start dealing with things ('Yeah') and you're up for it ('Yeah') that's really good, I'm really impressed. Well, shall we meet again in a week's time?

F   Yeah, at the same time.

Second Session (nine days later)

(They met by chance in the school reception area and Faisal had begun to talk on their way to the meeting room).

T So you were telling me there was a school governor's meeting yesterday.

F Yeah, 'cos I got excluded last time.

T That was before we met...

Yeah, a long time.

T   Since I met you the first time, what's been better since we met?

The therapist makes the immediate assumption that there will have been improvements since the first session.

F   The things normally I put off, I've tried it now. Lots of stuff goes through my mind, this one's been in there a long time, and before I go to sleep I said I'll think about it.

T   Yeah. What sorts of things have you been putting your mind to?

F   I have to say I haven't had a fag all day since I woke up, since I came to school.

T   Great.

F   I haven't had one! My friend asked me to, I go 'No'.

T   That's brilliant! *(shakes Faisal's hand).*

F   I'm happy with myself. I've been chewing gum, and that helps.

T   Right. So I asked what's been better, and no fags this morning. And you said something about putting your mind to things?

F   Yeah. My sister said this stuff was killing me.

T   Sister?

F   Yeah, she lives across the road from me, with my auntie.

T   You've got family around…

F   I've got a lot of family, cousins…

T   Can I ask you about that? Someone in the staff room this morning told me about the governor's meeting, and she said that no one from your family came.

This is another feature of working in an institution such as a school – the therapist is open to staff members bringing concerns to their attention. The therapist needs to decide quickly what to do with such information. Staff will assume that having told the therapist, it will then be 'dealt with'. Sometimes the therapist will accept this; usually they would have to check out whose responsibility for dealing with the issues it really is.

In the case of Faisal's family, although the concern was put to the therapist, he wasn't expected to resolve it. However, the therapist was sufficiently puzzled by it (given the comments Faisal had made about his family before) to want to raise it himself. This meant that if anything of serious concern arose from Faisal's replies, he would be duty-bound to tell him he would be reporting back. Such was not the case here.

F   Yeah. Nobody came. They were supposed to send a letter to my house, and the letter never came.

T   Ah.

F   Normally, I… er, normally, I… I'll tell you the truth now, normally when I get a bad letter, I'm the one who gets it and reads it, and I rip it up. But this time, I didn't get it! I looked everywhere for it, because I was expecting it to come. I told them. My family didn't believe me, 'There's no governor's meeting, you just want an excuse to come home late!' I said, 'No, I don't'.

T   I see. So, let's go back to my question, what's been better since last week? Keep on telling me.

F   I've been doing more healthier stuff.

T   Healthier stuff yeah, like what?

F   More football. More training. Usually, in the breaks I'm in the toilets smoking. Now I play football. Trying to get healthy.

T   Right. So you're not in the toilet smoking. You're out there being active.

F   Yeah.

T   Are you enjoying that? Is it good?

F   Yeah.

T   Do you feel the difference?

F   Yeah.

T   So, what else has been better?

F   Not running out of class.

T   So, not running out of class.

F   I admit I have done it but not as much as I used to.

T   Not as much. OK. Can you give me an example last week when you thought you would run out but you stopped yourself?

The therapist now moves from the general, 'What's better… what else has been better?' to a specific exception-seeking question.

F   My friend said let's go speak to them girls outside. They were outside the school and it was school time, they came to see us, and he said let's go see them. So I was about to… I got out of my seat, and said… you just got excluded, so… if I had gone out of the school I would probably have got excluded so I said no. I told him to wait. So I never went.

T   So he went out, and you stayed behind.

F   Yeah.

T   And you stayed in because you said, 'If I get caught I'm gonna get excluded again'.

F   Yeah.

T   But he still went! So how did you stop yourself from going with him?

F   I just, er, I just wanna, it feels like good I never got no letters from the school – I've been counting – it's been three weeks since I've been excluded, and not a single letter to say I been bad or anything like that. Even my Nan told...

T   What did she say?

F   Er, normally, she's checking the bills and there's always one with my name 'For the parents of Faisal', but she checks every day there's nothing there, nothing there, nothing there and she said to me, 'Have you been hiding them?' And I say, 'No. I swear...'

T   ...but you *have* been hiding them sometimes, so...

F   Yeah, before, before, before, but since then I haven't got no trouble, not a single one.

T   Since when? How long are we talking about?

F   Since I got excluded for that knife. Nothing to cause a detention or something like that, just to get a warning, no...

This is the first the therapist has heard about a knife! He decides to contain his surprise and curiosity. He thinks, 'So now I know why there was a governor's meeting!' but realises that to ask about all this would actually be irrelevant to the task at hand, and should stay focused on the progress made.

T   So another thing that's been different is that your Nan – did she actually say this to you the other day, 'There's been no letters?'

F   Yeah.

T   So what else has been different, in the last week?

F   Er, the way I speak, like I say too much rude words like 'fuck' and all that. I've calmed down. Usually I get so mad in a few minutes. I get angry in two minutes and start shouting around. Before I used to hit. I used to be worse before. If anybody got me so mad I used to hit them. Now, I swear, it's getting better. I swear at them but now it's going down. I ask them 'Why you doing that?' Yesterday my friend borrowed my Walkman. I told him not to give it to anyone but he did. I went to his house and said, 'Why did you do that?' I left. I have to control myself.

T   So how did you do it?

F   'Cos, usually I just open my mouth and start shouting. Now I bite my hand, I find it helps. And I count to ten. I've calmed down more.

T   So you count to ten and...

F   And I bite my finger. It seems weird but it works for me!

T   Well, you've heard the expression 'Put a sock in it' – so you've put a finger in it!

F   Yeah! It stops me getting mad.

T   Yeah. So you're finding ways to calm down, not running out of class as much…

F   Yeah, but some of these things I was doing before I met you…

T   Right, sure…

F   …but things like the smoking, that's…

T   …that's really different in the last week.

F   Yeah.

T   So even though some of these things obviously you were doing since before me, I'm still interested in the things you're doing more of now.

F   More. Hmm. Planning to do more homework.

T   *(writing)* 'Planning to do homework'.

F   I see my folder is more fuller than last week.

T   Yes, I can see it here! *(on table)*. What's in it?

F   Er, I have to do an essay on history… *(he describes the subject)*. Usually I wouldn't even be in class to hear the homework or even the lesson. I listened to the teacher for half an hour and then I went and got all the stuff for the essay ready. Usually I'd be in the toilets smoking or chasing around the girls.

T   So things really are different?

F   Yeah.

T   So the thing about homework and, er…

F   …more concentration.

T   More concentration, yeah. Who of the teachers would say they've noticed the changes the most, do you think?

F   Miss Hendry said I'm improved.

T   Brilliant!

F   Me, I'm a person that I definitely want to improve. People see I want to improve; they said I need help. I need help myself as well.

T   Hmm. *(pause)* So what do you reckon about the last week? Do you think it's been a good week?

The therapist senses that this would be a good point at which to take stock and assess the progress that's been made. He feels it probably has been very good, but he needs to let Faisal tell it as *he* sees it.

F   It feels good not to be in trouble! I get other trouble as well, not just in school, with my friends, 'cos they say to me, 'Let's go clubbing' and all this and all that. It feels good not worrying about getting dressed, getting going to club…

(There is an interruption. The next young person has arrived for their

…ession, and the therapist asks them to wait five minutes).

T   So it does feel like it's been a positive move for you in the last week. Good progress. What… if we think about the next week, what would be a sign for you of moving further forward?

F   Er, probably would be… lots of things, not smoking permanently, not going to clubs at weekends or going to less parties…

T   *Not* smoking altogether.

F   *Less* smoking – can't stop at once.

T   OK. Less clubs, and more of…

F   Homework.

T   Homework, what else? What are you going to do for *fun?*

F   For fun?

T   Yeah.

F   More football. I'm looking forward to that tomorrow. We've got a tournament.

T   Great. What else?

F   Come home more earlier. White shirt. Getting my stuff ready, iron the shirt. Normally I leave it for my Nan to do, but I could try to do it.

T   Good. So if I was a betting man, should I put money on it that you could achieve some of these things?

F   *Some* of them.

T   Some of them.

F   Yeah.

T   Let's be realistic here, right? *(laughs)*

F   Some of them. half of them, fifty-fifty. Smoking is hard for me because people really stress me out. It's like something I can run to. Before I used to just use violence but now that's something that helps me. Now I'm trying not to use that – use my mind to help myself. Before I just relied on cigarettes.

T   Yeah, so using your mind.

F   Yeah. Less relying on cigarettes.

T   It sounds like you've really made a start on that in this last week, like you say, putting your mind to things, getting your mind around things. No fags today, getting into football, resisting the invitation from your friend to go out of the school when it could have got you into trouble – that's brilliant, that really put your mind to it there. Planning to do more homework, more concentration, you've had feedback from Miss Hendry – she's seen improvement. It's looking…it's looking much better, isn't it?

Again, the therapist senses the importance of checking out *Faisal's* view of the changes, rather than simply assuming it's very positive. This seems to allow Faisal the space to express a fear.

F   Yeah, but something I'm scared, that I'm just going to do something silly and I'm gonna get excluded, it's my final, last chance.

T   Hmm.

F   And I'm really scared that I might get excluded. I don't want to but...

T   You're scared that you might do something...

F   Yeah, silly and I might get excluded, 'cos other schools might want to fight our school and if one of my friends has a fight with them I have to help my friend out. So I'm scared I might get excluded.

T   So am I right in saying that when you didn't go with your friend the other day, for example, that's like a little experiment in holding back from something?

F   Yeah.

T   'Cos if there's a fight and you have to support your friends, but if that's gonna be bad for you to get involved, you've got to make a decision that moment what's more important for you. Nobody can tell you, it will be down to you. But it sounds to me like you're getting a lot of practice at the moment in making decisions about what's right for you. It's preparation for when you're really tested, I suppose. But I hear you're worried, I hear that you're worried and...

The therapist has decided to take up a position of acknowledging the difficulty – the need to help friends out even in a fight – and to focus on Faisal's ability to 'make decisions about what's right for you'. It may, he implies, mean doing what's not right for his friends.

F   Yeah. I really don't wanna get excluded.

T   Sure.

F   I've been excluded before and I didn't like it.

T   No.

F   'Cos I had to work in a shop that I didn't like.

T   But do you think if you can progress in the way you're going now, if you keep this going this will help...

F   I told my friend, 'Don't get in any fights'.

T   Yeah.

F   I don't want to lose my education for some silly fight. But, I said, if it comes to that I'll help you but don't do something silly, for no reason.

T   Yeah.

These fights are serious. People are angry at each other.

T   Look, I know that we've got to stop today. Umm. I hear that you're determined, but worried, so you're not being silly about this and you're not saying, 'Oh yeah, it's all crap, we've done it now'. There's still work to be done. What we could do is meet next Tuesday…

Outcome

Faisal was not at school the following Tuesday, and the school did not book any further meetings.

Follow-up eight months later – half way through the next academic year – revealed that Faisal had not been excluded on any further occasion. While not a 'model' pupil, he was seen as a success case, especially given the fact that he had initially come to the school as a boy permanently excluded from his previous school.

Unfortunately, a serious family crisis occurred shortly after this follow-up and Faisal's behaviour began to deteriorate. Other agencies were involved and the school did not inform the therapist until Faisal had been permanently excluded for a serious incident in which he himself had not been violent but had been sufficiently implicated to warrant this drastic action.

The school's view was that events in Faisal's life outside school had had an overwhelming influence on him and that they could see no way that therapy could have made a difference to these different circumstances. Whether or not further intervention from the brief therapist *would* have helped will never be known. The school's view was that, given his record prior to joining the school, Faisal had had a settled period of schooling that had enabled him, in his words, to 'surprise' himself with what he was capable of, and to realise that 'this is possible for me'. While left with a feeling of sadness regarding the longer term outcome to this case, the therapist is hopeful that some of what Faisal learned regarding his possibilities will stay with him into the future.

The outcome is, perhaps, a reminder of what everyone in the field of education is only too aware, namely that, however hard they try to make school a nurturing and supportive environment, there are always factors beyond their control, and that 'failure' is often something that has to be put in a wider perspective.

Finding motivation

In the case described above, Faisal came to the first session prepared to acknowledge that changes were needed in his behaviour if he was to be able to remain in school. In many situations, however, the student only superficially, if at all, acknowledges the need to make changes. Many will claim that the school *is* being 'unfair' to them in its demands.

Whether or not the school is being unfair does not have to be an issue for the therapist. Exploring what a fair school would look like nearly always draws out a parallel picture of a fair student. However, where a student has complained about a relationship with a particular member of staff, and in subsequent sessions has still not been able to effect sufficient change in the relationship, then one option for the therapist is to talk to an appropriate person with managerial status to ascertain the best way forward. In some cases this might lead to direct intervention by the Head of the Department concerned or has paved the way for a meeting between the therapist and a teacher which has taken the form of a consultation. Further options that have been used on rare occasions have been meetings with parents and even with peers.

The most significant connection the therapist has made with the wider system of the school has been through requesting feedback on any positive changes that the school has noticed in a student's behaviour subsequent to each session. This has perhaps encouraged members of staff to be on the look out for even the smallest signs of progress in the students they know have been referred. During his nearly two years in the school, the therapist has noticed a decrease in the number of students complaining that 'When I'm good nobody notices – they only notice when they think I'm being bad'.

Even though most of the young people appear to feel they *have* to attend the therapy session, it is usually possible to identify a goal that suits them. To the question, 'What are your best hopes for this meeting?' many will shrug their shoulders and say they 'don't know', but most have agreed that they or the school are unhappy with the situation. Asked if they would prefer things to be happier for them in school, most of them have answered 'Yes'. They then have the start of a goal.

Once a goal has been identified, the questions that follow are focused on finding out how the young person will know that things are better for them *and for the school.* The questions are never only one thing or the other, except temporarily. That is, the therapist neither focuses exclusively on the young person's ideas of what they want for themselves nor explores only what the student thinks the school expects. It has sometimes been our experience that much younger children, such as five-year-olds, tend to express the future in terms of what they've learned adults want of them. But older children are quite capable of expressing both sides.

There are, of course, a few cases where the student continues to say 'don't know' or even 'don't care'. In such cases the therapist checks if the student knows what the consequences of no-change would be, such as permanent exclusion or transfer to a pupil referral unit, and if they care about such consequences. When the response to *that* has still been 'No', the therapist has become curious as to what the young person's preferred outcome would be – even if that has entailed a discussion of what they would do outside their current school. For example, if a student said their aim was to be moved to another school, they would then be encouraged to say how things would be different in the new environment: how would they cope with the stresses and strains *there?* It is then a small step to looking at the ways they have of coping in their current school. It becomes a case of distinguishing 'means' and 'ends' (Ratner, 1998): for example, if the young person hates school work but hopes to get a well paid job in future, then the 'means' to achieving that are most likely to be through doing some school work first! There are of course a number of 'ends' that school can satisfy in a young person's life, even if they claim not to care about education itself. A small number of students, for example, are concerned to protect their parents from being the subject of telephone calls from and meetings with education professionals (and also to protect themselves from parental wrath!). Their goal then becomes that of sustaining or promoting harmony at home, the 'means' to which are to find ways of coping with life at school.

Inevitably, there will occasionally be cases where a young person is emphatic that there is nothing that school can offer them as a means to achieving other goals. They may identify some other issue to discuss that seems appropriate, such as a concern at home; some young women have talked about their self-harming activities such as cutting themselves. Otherwise there is probably little the therapist can do, and therapy will have to be brought to a halt. This has not happened in the project, but then it is unlikely that such a young person would ever have been persuaded to meet a therapist in the first case. What has happened on rare occasions is that the student persists in being disgruntled with education, but recognises that they have little option but to continue to attend – usually due to parental pressure, a different 'end', as referred to above – and then the goal of the therapy is to find the student's ways of *coping*. In time, a different goal may emerge. A 14-year-old young woman (not seen in this project) once said, in answer to the 'miracle question', she would become 16 years old, so that she wouldn't have to go to school. Asked what she would do then, she described a life of independent working and living. The therapist validated these aims as reasonable and realistic but acknowledged that, sadly, he did not have a way to make her miracle come about overnight! Consequently he asked her how she would cope for the next two years until she could be more independent, and enquired how she might use the next two years to 'practice' becoming more independent in her life: the means to achieving an end that was right for her *and* for others.

The observations made above demonstrate our view, as expressed in chapter two, that motivation is not some fixed quality that a young person either has or – more usually, in many people's minds! – has not. Our experience over the years, and most especially in the school project, has convinced us that all clients have goals and are motivated towards some positive end. An interesting impression the therapist has gained over the course of the project, in contrast to the usual view of the counselling 'relationship', is that apparently dismissive non-verbal behaviour is best not interpreted as lack of motivation. Whether the young person yawns, avoids eye contact, fidgets endlessly, sprawls in their chair or even spends half the session walking around the room playing football with a ball of paper, rarely have these apparent signs of non co-operation been found to have much predictive value with regard to outcome. The same can be said about 'articulateness': whether the young person cannot seem to complete sentences of more than two syllables, or elaborates their reply for five minutes non-stop, rarely has any bearing on outcome. This is not to say that the therapist can simply disregard such behaviour if it is particularly disruptive to the interview. The only criterion is whether the young person is paying any attention whatsoever to the questions asked, and clearly some are able to do this even while moving about the room. As many practitioners will know, young people constantly stretch the limits of conventional counselling 'rules' and are a great spur to our powers of creativity... and endurance!

Acknowledgements

Running a counselling project in a school can be a mammoth task. The therapist has felt at times that he's had the easiest job, to just show up, talk to some kids and go! Meanwhile, the school has had to arrange that the room is kept free of other activities for that morning, that teachers of the students to be seen are aware of their forthcoming absence from a lesson, and that the students are themselves informed. Sometimes, despite all the preparation, a student forgets, and the therapist has oured corridors and classrooms to ferret out the young person concerned – but it is just as likely that someone will respond to the lost-looking therapist and do the hunting for him. And on top of it all, the therapist asks to receive feedback on each of the students before seeing them again!

In South Camden Community School, almost all this work has been undertaken by Carolyn Kain, Head of Learning Development, to whom the therapist is deeply indebted. He is also grateful to Nicola Mansfield and Johanna Fitzgerald, who had the idea for the project in the first place.

CHAPTER SEVEN

OTHER CLINICAL APPLICATIONS

OLDER PEOPLE

Of the older people seen, the commonest issue for this group has been the wish to establish a closer relationship with 'offspring'. One of the very first clients was a woman wishing to reunite with her daughter. The client was a Holocaust survivor and her fifty-year-old daughter lived in Berlin. It was understandably the last place the client wanted to go, yet it was the only place she could meet her daughter. The case was the team's first clear failure. The therapist had not yet learned to temper his enthusiasm for the 'positive' and after three sessions the client withdrew saying such positive thinking was not helpful. The therapist wrote to acknowledge respect for her decision and hoped that she would find a path to her daughter. He concluded with, 'And if you do get to Berlin, send me a card!'

Six weeks later came a card from Berlin saying only, 'All is well.'

Any therapeutic approach tends to work well with older people, who, with so much experience to draw on, often need very little help to move forward in their lives. But a solution focus is particularly effective given its antidote effect on ageism. There are numerous beliefs and rules at an individual, familial and social level which serve to deny and undermine the competence of older people. By consistently working in the opposite direction, seeking out and identifying competence, solution focused therapy can quickly release the normal solution finding abilities of older people, and a very little therapy can go a long way.

A white woman in her eighties was referred following a serious suicide attempt. The referrer saw the client as 'untreatable' but referred her as a last resort. The client was in a chronic state of worry about her daughter's attitude to her and said her husband treated her like a slave. When he died she was going to kill herself properly. He was eighty-six. She said neither daughter nor husband would come to the sessions since they had had family therapy before. Over five sessions the therapist and client discovered numerous ways she was able to influence her husband and numerous ways the daughter showed love and respect for her mother. Once the existing exceptions had been elicited the client began to create new ones for herself. The goal she had set ('How will you know when things have really changed?') was to have a family party to celebrate her husband's 87th birthday. Shortly after the party she wrote to the therapist saying that her daughter had suddenly changed and therefore she did not need help any more!

This sudden change was a surprise but not untypical. Though many exceptions were discovered during the five sessions they had seemed to remain just that – exceptions. However, if they had been sufficient to change the client's way of being with her daughter, then the daughter's behaviour would also change. The fact that the client had not appeared to notice her own changed behaviour suggests that whatever she did was entirely consistent with her view of herself – she must simply have been doing more of something she was already doing or had the potential to do. But when she saw her daughter change she was ready to accept the change as real and respond to it affirmatively.

GROUP WORK

We have worked with groups in a number of different settings, including client groups and staff groups.

In general we have found that solution focused interventions, such as future focused questions, are particularly applicable to group settings. In one group of three black and one white women, asked to identify a goal, all chose aspects of their 'partner' relationships – two wanted their partners to stop beating them up, one wanted her ex-partner to stop pestering her and one wanted her husband to stop treating her like a slave.

Much of that session was spent talking about the different ways they had of keeping themselves safe from stronger, aggressive men. This was not to say that the violence they suffered was of their own making. Rather, given the unfair circumstances, what could they do to redress the balance? It turned out that they all had ways to diminish the level of risk that they were living with and, what is more, they all had ideas about untried ways of keeping safe – some of them involving dire consequences for the aggressor! The woman not subject to physical violence was rather left out of this discussion, but when she was asked, 'And how will you know when your husband begins to change his attitude towards you?', she replied: 'When he makes me a cup of tea!' We discovered that he always ordered her to make tea and the next time he did it would be that evening when he came in from work. It was suggested to Elaine, the group member in question, that she 'do something different' at that point… 'anything you like, crazy or sane, as long as it's different'.

A week later Elaine reported gleefully that she'd received her first cup of tea in fourteen years of marriage. When the group ended around three months later, none of the women were experiencing violence at home. One year later the most assaulted of the women (she had on two separate occasions needed major abdominal and brain surgery after beatings) felt herself safe and in charge of her life, and was taking a computer course.

These were dramatic results, partly accounted for by plain good luck. Because of his interest in domestic violence the therapist was contacted by a reporter for *Panorama* who then met the group. The group members felt greatly supported by this interest which furthered their transition from 'victims' to 'survivors'. Rather than talk about abuse, they spoke about what they had done to stop it and what the police and others could do to help. One of the women became the star of the show, the programme starting and ending with her words. The interview with *Panorama* had embedded the new thinking that was developing in the group, putting these women in touch with the power of the exceptions to the daily rule of their lives. And they turned the exceptions into a new rule.

We have facilitated several groups of women who are survivors of incest. The very act of participating in a group has itself been empowering for many of the women. This is true for many group settings – for example, substance misusers and people living with mental health difficulties report that they often gain much from groups where they can share experiences with others who are more likely to 'understand' what they have been through. It may be more so for people who have survived traumas that they feel they cannot disclose to others for fear of how other people might react: most have experienced the pain of being blamed and rejected all too often. The sense of sharing and understanding that can build up between survivors can be a very great resource. In one group, at the end of a meeting the participants spent longer talking with each other, *after* the group had ended and the facilitators had left, than the session itself had lasted.

This means, of course, that in groups there is considerable 'problem talk' as participants seek to share their experiences with others. Just as in individual therapy, the solution focused practitioner will not regard 'problem talk' as counter-productive as long as it appears to enable clients to feel acknowledged and validated in their life experiences. The therapist needs to judge when the conversation has gone beyond a valuable sharing and created instead a negative set that will pull people down; skill is then needed in inviting participants into a conversation focusing more on resources and strengths. This is frequently harder in ne group setting, where the therapist usually has less influence than they might feel they have in individual sessions. Nevertheless, in the group the worker can use the presence of others as a resource for the stuck individual to draw on: 'Who else here has had to deal with what Mary has experienced? What have you found helpful in dealing with this?' We have found that groups have generated ideas on issues such as how to resist the urge to cut oneself, ways of resisting a partner's demand for sex, and how to keep yourself safe when meeting new people in social situations.

We have found that, in staff group consultations, scale questions are particularly valuable. In smaller groups, asking people to guess where they think another person will rate themselves, before that person gets to answer the question himself or herself has proved a source of useful discussion in some groups. However, the consultant has to be sensitive to people's vulnerability in such situations. If it is even remotely possible that someone might feel unsafe in disclosing their scale assessment, they are not asked to talk about that – but to talk about how they will know things have moved on from the scale rating that they have kept secret to themselves.

CONTROL PROBLEMS WITH YOUNG CHILDREN

Unless parents can maintain some control of their children, solution focused therapy, which depends on talking, can be hopelessly disrupted. However, if the therapist, in response to the noise, takes an advisory or executive position, the co-operative basis of the therapy is endangered. Our approach is to ask parents to consider, while the child is acting badly, what methods they have used in the past that have worked, and to use them again in the session; if control is still not being achieved, then they are asked to try something different. Our position will be to support the parent(s) with as much praise as possible, based on our belief that they can manage to gain control. If we do decide to make a suggestion, it will be offered in a very tentative form, worded as closely as possible to what is felt might be natural to this particular parent, e.g. 'Do you think it would help if you were to hold her?' 'Do you think it would help if you and your wife were to make a "choir" and sing together on this one?' In our experience our advice is usually rejected and the parents proceed to their own solution, unless the 'advice' is offered in such a general way, preferably in the form of a question, that the family can make it their own. In the case of a ten-year-old Bangladeshi boy, Kamal, whose challenge to his father's authority had led him into danger, Kamal's defiance of his father in-session led his father to take a rope and tie his hands in a bid to control him. The therapist, also acting in the role of Child Protection Worker, approached the mother, and through an interpreter said that he could see that she was not happy that her husband had had to resort to such drastic methods. What ideas did she have to resolve the difficulty? Using no words the mother untied Kamal, resolved the confrontation between the boy and his father by dressing Kamal, and Kamal agreed to go out with his father as the father had required.

There are no doubt a number of explanations for the sequence of events described above, and why the mother only felt able to act when the white, male social worker gently empowered her to do so. But perhaps the crucial element was the message being conveyed to the family, that 'This family can do things differently.'

UNPREDICTABLE DISASTERS

A problem of a different kind can arise when a client comes to a session and reports that some unpredictable disaster has occurred between sessions. A single, white male client (age 34) was being seen for help with his social isolation and feelings of depression. Therapy had progressed steadily, with the client making slow progress in relation to getting work and increasing his social life. Then, at the start of the sixth session, he reported that his 72-year-old father had died less than two weeks previously. He described himself as not feeling anything, feeling numb, bereft and lost. He said one of his sisters had thrown herself into her work, and he talked about some of his own work plans. The therapist put it to the client that his reactions to his loss were perfectly natural, and he could use the session to talk about his bereavement, and how he would get support now he felt so bereft and alone, or he could talk about how he could keep things going, particularly with respect to his work plans. He replied, 'I feel now father's gone I don't have to live up to him any more. I can really… try to live my own level which is not as high as his.' He said he wanted to follow his sister, to do more than ever: 'I want so much going on so that I can't think about it.' He didn't see this as avoiding what had happened; he felt it was the right way to move forward and consequently the therapist followed his lead and the discussion then centred on the precise details of his work progress. The task that was given to him at the end of the session went as follows: 'When you're able to go to your father's grave, without preparing in advance what you're going to say, tell him what you need to say so that you will be free to rise to your own level'. When he returned for his next session, he brought with him a long letter that he had written to his father and which he planned to read to him when he was able to visit the grave. It was a moving document that contained elements of appreciation but consisted mainly of disappointments and resentments, and hope for the future that he could now get on with his own life. He told the therapist that he was working harder than ever. He made this his last session.

VIOLENCE

Domestic violence, the physical abuse of women by their male partners, is an issue that presents a particular challenge. The question that keeps confronting us is how we can help a woman through therapy without exposing her to greater risk, to the risk for example, of being attacked for views expressed in therapy. We have seen a number of such cases that have necessitated certain changes to our more usual style of solution focused work.

A consistent feature of our work in this area is that, contrary to our usual practice of letting clients lead us in terms of the goals for therapy, in cases where it is clear or we suspect a woman to be at risk we unilaterally put the woman's safety at the top of the agenda for therapy. In the case of violent men, we place control of their violence at the heart of our work with them. If this priority is not accepted by the man then we would discontinue therapy. We also find ourselves having to be cautious about any exceptions or changes that clients report to us. Instead of 'cheering on change' as we would usually do, we consider that when women who have endured prolonged periods of violent abuse report improvements, we need to be encouraging but also realistic about whether these will lead to increased safety in the long-term or not. The sort of questions we might therefore ask are:

'How much safer does that make you?'
'Would you say that that made you safer or left you more at risk?'
'What will your partner think? Will his thinking that make you less safe?'
It sometimes appears to us that the most obvious solution to the problem of repeated assault is for the woman to leave her partner. We are aware that this is our view, and so we are careful to elicit the client's view of what is best for her. We will help the client weigh up the options available to her, paying particular attention to her safety. Our constant question is: how can we help this person stay safe while respecting her autonomy?

In one case a woman came to therapy with a badly bruised face and a justifiable fear that her husband might kill her if she tried to stop being his 'slave'; she believed he would violently object to her seeking therapy. After four sessions of painstaking concern with the details of minimising risk in a very dangerous situation the client found the strength to leave her husband (they had been 'together' for nineteen years). At the fifth session she reported having taken out a non-molestation order, persuaded her husband to accept therapy with her and returned to him. Because they wanted to 'start afresh' they were going to see a new therapist together.

Three months later she wrote a 'deeply felt thank you' saying 'I was moved by your concern for my well-being, physical and psychological'. She also reported that he had 'never raised a finger against me' since their reconciliation.

In the case of the Vaneks, the couple were seen separately after Mr. Vanek had tried to strangle his wife. The agenda agreed for Mrs. Vanek was how she might keep safe in future, and for Mr. Vanek how he might control his violence. When the couple reunited, Mr. Vanek was asked to make a commitment to non-violence, which he did. However, the relationship between them again deteriorated. The request for a commitment to non-violence was repeated by the therapist, but Mr. Vanek refused, saying he knew he was about to lose control. The therapist immediately switched the conversation to a consideration of Mrs. Vanek's safety, and what 'escape plans' (White and Epston, 1990) might be available to her. They were adamant that there was only one way – that they separate, which they did.

Mrs. Vanek continued to be seen on her own (the therapist heard nothing further from her husband), and an issue she raised has led to a further adaptation of our approach.

Mrs. Vanek remained oppressed by thoughts of concern for her husband and the hope that he would return to her so that she could help him with the 'sickness', as she called his propensity for violence. It seemed clear to us that these thoughts would hold her back from making a life for herself, and would make her vulnerable to danger from her husband if he should return to her in the future.

We have found that when clients appear to be consistently stuck in a particular thought or behaviour pattern, then Michael White's notion of the 'externalising of the problem' is very helpful (White and Epston, 1990). It involves depicting with the client the control the problem has over their lives, as if it were 'out there', even outside of themselves. In this case, Mrs. Vanek readily admitted that she was the prey of 'false dreams' of a good life with her husband. These false dreams, the therapist argued, were getting in the way of her living her own life. He suggested that the false dreams liked it when she missed her husband, or felt sorry for him, or dreamed of an unreal future with him. He then asked her what the false dreams did not like, and she said, 'They don't like me being happy, or the idea of my getting a job, or of taking driving lessons.' Now there suddenly appeared to her a way forward, a way to defy the oppressive false dreams in her life. As for the driving lessons, this was the first mention she had ever made. This spontaneous 'exception' would appear to justify White's thesis about 'externalising the problem', that in the act of talking about a problem as being an object or creature that controls the client from outside, then the client can distance herself from it and begin to reclaim her life from it. The idea of driving lessons, based on her new-found determination to be really independent of her husband, provided the therapist with a useful metaphor for future use: questions could now be framed in terms of whether she was still a passenger in her life, or had she at last moved into the driving seat?

WORKING WITH PEOPLE WHO MISUSE DRUGS AND ALCOHOL

Work with substance misusers has been a particular challenge to adopting a solution focused approach, as standard notions in the field include beliefs that the problem is an 'illness' and that clients can only begin recovery having acknowledged that control is beyond them. The field also assumes that it is important to focus on the particular substance that is being misused and its effects on the user. In our solution focused approach 'It has been found that there is little need to distinguish between the types of substances being used.' (Ratner and Yandoli, 1996).

Our approach, first and foremost, is one of acceptance: acceptance of the client's view of their problem (whether they see it as an 'addiction' or a temporary loss of control), and consequently acceptance of their goals (whether they may be abstinence or controlled use in future). In the spirit of acceptance we are also willing to work with clients who are drink or drug affected, provided of course that it is safe to work with them as they are.

We have found that, as in all cases, very careful attention needs to be paid to the detail of clients' preferred futures. 'Not drinking to excess', for example, is a typical wish but is not, in itself, a goal. Encouraging clients to depict, in detail, what they will be doing when they are no longer using or when they have the problem under control sometimes leads to a realisation of the considerable changes that the client will have to make in their life. The client, sometimes, decides that the changes needed are too hard for them at the particular time. They are not, for example, ready to change their lifestyle or their friends, even though they have described a future in which it is precisely these things that will have to be different if the future is to be less problem dominated than it is at present. The lure of having more money when drug usage has stopped, and better health, is sometimes an incentive but not always a strong one. For others, awareness of the costs of not changing, such as broken relations, loss of contact with children and further imprisonment, are too great to bear. Scale questions related to a person's confidence in change, and their willingness to make an effort, will help in the task of drawing out a person's motivation to make changes.

In particular, a focus on exceptions, the times a person resists the urge to misuse, is a key to someone feeling encouraged to take more control of a situation they may feel is beyond them. In solution focused work a 'drinks diary', a common task in the field, is adapted to encouraging the client to note what they do to cope on the occasions they use *less*, in other words, a 'resisting the urge' diary.

Relapse is of course, a common occurrence and it is essential to encourage clients to move from a position of self-blame and shame to reviewing ways they have come out of relapses in the past and how they will know they are recovering this time. This way they may stay focused on what they do when they aren't using. It is, as de Shazer has said, harder to stop something happening, as in trying to prevent relapses, than it is to start or maintain doing something else.

In one case, a woman who had severe binge drinking episodes that had led to her daughter becoming the concern of Social Services, had no confidence (0 on the scale) in not having further binges. Asking her to notice what she did to stop having binges was a failure. The binges only started to reduce in length and severity when she was asked to notice what she did as she *came out* of binges.

In cases where clients seem stuck, the usual solution focused procedure of reviewing the client's coping strategies, and exploring possible small steps forward, is maintained. There are occasional situations where clients are able to be quite clear about the steps they need to – and believe they can – take to move forward, but each session sees them complaining that 'nothing's changed'. In some cases we have suggested that, 'For now, we won't make another appointment. Please call us for another meeting when you have begun to make changes.' This puts the matter back to the client, implying that they will make changes when they are ready to do so. Some clients call having made changes; in some cases we haven't heard further from the clients, and don't know if that means 'success' or that they have been referred elsewhere. Either way it prevents us getting caught up in seeing people over and over again with few signs of obvious progress. The adage, 'If it ain't working, do something different', is the golden rule here!

RESEARCH STUDIES
AND FOLLOW-UP

The reasons for the growth of solution focused brief therapy over the past ten years are complex. However, it is incontrovertible that the enormous interest shown by practitioners seems to be associated significantly with the extent to which the approach fits well with the current emphasis on equal opportunities. In addition, practitioners report positively on their experience of using the approach and the way in which it is regarded by them as empowering of clients. Repeated reports that use of solution focused brief therapy seems to energise the worker rather than drain their energy seem to further explain the phenomenon of its continued and growing attractiveness (Miller et al, 1997).

The growth of the approach has not just been driven by the preoccupations of practitioners, and indeed it could not have happened without the sympathetic support of managers and funders. For managers in funded services, and increasingly for a more informed and 'empowered' group of potential clients, the key questions relate to effectiveness and value for money. Does it work and how long does it take? 'Evidence-based practice' is now a familiar phrase and audit studies are now more widely expected by managers and funders. It is the evidence of effectiveness and brevity which has led managers to support the continued and growing influence of the approach through the commissioning of training in solution focused brief therapy.

In relation to most newly established approaches, research activity is typically phased. The first phase is characterised by simple customer satisfaction studies: did clients get what they wanted when they came to therapy? There are a number of studies listed below that fall into this category (De Jong and Hopwood, 1996) (de Shazer, 1991) (Iveson, 1991) (Parslow, 1993). In the second phase, in addition to further satisfaction surveys, there begin to be studies that use control groups and 'before and after' measures. Sometimes this involves using standard questionnaires that have been tested across a number of studies (Eakes et al, 1997), (Sundman, 1997) (Zimmerman et al, 1996) and (Zimmerman et al, 1997). This phase is also marked by the testing of outcomes against hard indicators of change, for example, re-offending rates (Linforss and Magnusson, 1997), (Uken, 1998) or getting back to work (Cockburn, 1997). The third phase of research tends to involve comparing the effectiveness of an approach in comparison with other approaches, often with the addition of a control group and in relation to a particular problem area. In relation to solution focused brief therapy there are studies from the first and the second phases and none as yet from the third research phase. Naturally as an approach is more established the length of follow-up studies tends to extend. The longest follow-up study so far looking at the application of solution focused brief therapy is a five-year study (Isebaert, 1997).

Summarising the findings, the studies show that the standard demographic variables – gender, age, race and class – make no significant difference to outcome. Indeed, neither does the mix of gender, race or age of client and therapist – same or different – make a difference. In addition the studies show no significant difference in outcome in relation to the nature of the problem. De Jong and Hopwood (1996) in their study divided problem presentations into 22 different categories that showed little variation. Although some of the studies have shown chronicity (the length of time that the problem has persisted prior to therapy) not to be significant, McDonald's two studies (1994 and 1997) do show an association between outcome and chronicity. A number of the studies listed below are process studies, looking at the experience of the client and the therapist (Metcalf and Thomas, 1994), or at the way that the therapeutic conversation is constructed (Gale and Newfield, 1992). Further studies look at specific elements of the therapeutic process (Beyebach and Carranza, 1997), (Gingerich, de Shazer and Weiner-Davis, 1988), (Weiner-Davis, de Shazer and Gingerich, 1987), (Adams, Piercey and Jurich, 1991).

The current position, and of course knowledge is constantly developing, is that the research shows good outcomes of between 65% and 83% across a range of referrals. However, it is not yet clear for whom the approach is effective and for whom it is not. The only assessment therefore that makes sense is to try utilising solution focused brief therapy and to discover in that process whether it makes a difference. If it does not then the onus is on the worker to 'try something different', whatever that might be.

STUDIES

Adams, J., Piercey, F., Jurich, J. (1991) **Effects of Solution Focused Therapy's 'Formula First Session Task' on Compliance and Outcome in Family Therapy**. *Journal of Marital and Family Therapy*. 17(3)

Positive impact on co-operation compared with problem-focused task and associated with more clients reporting their situation improved in the second session.

Beyebach, M., Carranza, E. (1997) **Therapeutic interaction and drop-out: measuring relational communications in solution focused therapy.** *Journal of Family Therapy* 19(2) 173 – 212.
Study looking at patterns of communication within therapy that are associated with the client continuing. More conflictual patterns of communications associated with drop-out.

Cockburn, Jack T. (1997) **Solution-focused therapy and psychosocial adjustment to orthopaedic rehabilitation in a work hardening program.** *Journal of Occupational Rehabilitation* 7 (2) 97-106
This study used the rigorous 'Solomon four groups' design in a clinical setting and found that within 60 days following SFT 68% of the treated clients had returned to work compared with only 4% of the control clients, who had received standard rehab treatment. The study was conducted at the Lewisville Rehabilitation Center in Lewisville, Texas. (Thanks to Wallace Gingerich for this summary).

De Jong, P., Hopwood, L. (1996) **From the home of solution-focused therapy: Outcome Research on Treatment conducted at the Brief Family Therapy Center, 1992 – 1993**. In Miller, S. et al (Eds.) *Handbook of Brief Therapy*. San Francisco: Jossey-Bass
Study involving 275 clients. Average attendance 2.9 sessions (3.7 for those whose goals were met, 2.9 for 'some' progress and 2.3 for no progress). Follow-up at 7/9 months. 77% good outcome on self-rating. Very wide range of 'problem presentations'. The problems included depression, suicidal thoughts, anxiety, panic attacks, sleep problems, eating disorders, withdrawn behaviour, health problems, alcohol and other drug abuse, job-related problems, financial concerns, parent-child conflict, communication problems, family violence, sexual abuse, physical abuse, marital and relationship problems, sexual problems, bereavement, self-esteem problems, sibling problems and blended-family issues.

de Shazer, S. (1991) *Putting Difference to Work*. New York: Norton.
The appendix of this book contains a summary of two unpublished studies carried out by Kiser (Kiser, 1988) (Kiser and Nunnally, 1990) at the Brief Family Therapy Center in Milwaukee. 86% good outcome at 18 months within an average of 4.6 sessions. Clients who came to more sessions report better outcomes than those who came to fewer.

Eakes, G., Walsh, S., Markowski, M et al (1997) **Family-centred brief solution focused therapy with chronic schizophrenia: a pilot study.** *Journal of Family Therapy* 19 (2) 145-158.
Study with control group receiving 'traditional out-patient therapy'. Test group received 5 sessions over 10-week period. Significant differences found in expressiveness, active-recreational orientation, moral-religious emphasis and family incongruence. Encouraging results demonstrating the need for expanded studies.

Gale, J., Newfield, N. (1992) **A Conversation Analysis of a Solution-Focused Marital Therapy Session.** *Journal of Marital and Family Therapy,* 18 (2), 153 – 167.
Detailed analysis of single session with a couple. The therapist was Bill O'Hanlon.

Gingerich, W., de Shazer, S., Weiner-Davis, M. (1988) **Constructing Change: A Research View of Interviewing.** In. Lipchik, E. (ed.) *Interviewing.* (21-31) Rockville. Maryland. Aspen.
Study examining transcripts to identify clients' responses to 'change-talk'. Study found that client changes were most likely to occur after therapist used change related talk.

Isebaert, L. (1997) Unpublished study. Reported at EBTA conference. Bruges.
This study looks at outcomes over a five-year period of working with problem drinkers at the St John Hospital in Bruges. Some were treated on an outpatient basis only, some in-patient and some a mixture of both. Clients could choose best way to work for them. Variety of goals accepted: total abstinence, controlled drinking, reduced drinking or 'feast-day' drinking. Average length of in-patient treatment 2 weeks, average number of outpatient sessions 4.5. 75% either abstinent (50%) or controlled drinking (25%) at 5 years. Of those still drinking 79% reported that no one now saw drinking as a problem. 80% no further treatment since discharge. Results confirmed by spouse/police/other.

Iveson, D. (1991) Unpublished dissertation. Institute of Family Therapy/Birkbeck College
A follow-up study completed in 1991. In this sample 83% of the clients involved reported improvement and the average number of sessions was 4.7.

Linforss, L., Magnusson, D. (1997) **Solution focused therapy in prison.** *Contemporary Family Therapy* 19 (1) 89 – 104
Study with matched control group in prison working with high

recidivist offenders, most of whom were narcotics users. Average number of sessions was 5. Follow-up to 16 months. Differences in re-offending rate, seriousness of subsequent offences, survival.

MacDonald, A. J. (1994) **Brief therapy in adult psychiatry.** *Journal of Family Therapy,* 16: 415 – 426.
A study which looks at the application of Brief Therapy in a Psychiatric Service in a hospital in Scotland. 70% good outcome. Average 3.7 sessions.

MacDonald, A. (1997) **Brief therapy in adult psychiatry – further outcomes.** *Journal of Family Therapy* 19(2) 213 – 222.
Follow-up on further sample of 36 clients seen within mental health setting. Good outcome in 64% of cases. Social class not a significant variable in outcome. Replication, largely, of earlier study findings.

McKeel, A. J. (1996) **A clinician's guide to research on solution focused brief therapy.** In Miller, S. et al (Eds.) *Handbook of Brief Therapy.* San Francisco: Jossey-Bass.
A review of the research findings available.

Metcalf, L., Thomas, F. (1994) **Client and therapist perceptions of solution-focused brief therapy: A qualitative analysis.** *Journal of Family Psychotherapy.* (5) 49 – 66.
This study interviews both therapists and their clients about their experience of solution focused brief therapy.

Miller, Scott, Duncan, Barry, and Hubble, Mark (1997) *Escape from Babel: Toward a unifying language for psychotherapy practice.* New York: Norton.
Text examining the literature on effective practice in psychotherapy and moving towards the identification of key areas for the practitioner to bear in mind.

Parslow, S. (1993) Unpublished dissertation. Institute of Family Therapy/Birkbeck College.
A follow-up study of solution focused work in a Drug Dependency Unit in London. This was a very small pilot study, involving just 11 clients. 91.7% of these reported that their complaint was better. The average number of sessions here was 2.3 and all the clients completed in under 6 sessions.

Shilts, L., Filippino, C. Nau, D. S. (1994) **Client-informed therapy.** *Journal of Systemic Therapies.* 13: 39-52.
Focus on the development of co-operation.

Sundman P. (1997) **Solution focused ideas in Social Work.** *Journal of*

Family Therapy 19(2) 159 – 172.

Work compared of social workers who had had short training in solution focused brief therapy, and work of workers using 'traditional' means. Clients in the test group were more satisfied with their outcomes, social workers from test group 'did' less for clients and clients in the test group were more active themselves.

Uken, A. (1998) **Unpublished study.** *Reported at EBTA conference, Salamanca.*

Groupwork diversion project with men convicted of battering their partners. Compulsory attendance (or prison). Re-offending rates significantly lower than those of offenders allocated to more traditional therapeutic approaches (17% as opposed to 40-60%). Participants are reported to show significant levels of co-operation, enthusiasm and express more hope and optimism. Briefer treatment than problem-focused approaches.

Weiner-Davis, M., de Shazer, S., Gingerich, W. (1987) **Constructing the Therapeutic Solution by Building on Pretreatment Change: an Exploratory Study.** *Journal of Family and Marital Therapy.* 13(4):359-63.

Study examining the rate of occurrence of pre-treatment change and considering the effectiveness of different opening questions in eliciting client reports of such change.

Zimmerman, T. S., Jacobsen, R. B., MacIntyre, M., Watson, C. (1996) **Solution focused parenting groups: An empirical study.** *Journal of Family Therapy* 19(2) 159 – 172.

Parents of adolescents randomly assigned to test (30) group and control (12) group. Test group received six-week group. Post-group significant differences in Parenting Skills Inventory (PSI).

Zimmerman, T. S., Prest, L., Wetzel, B. (1997) **Solution focused couples therapy groups: an empirical study.** *Journal of Family Therapy 19(2)* 125-144.

Study with control group of 23 treatment group couples in 6-week solution focused group programme. Differences reported by couples and significant pre-post-group differences noted in Dyadic Adjustment Scale (DAS).

READING

The literature relating to solution focused brief therapy has expanded substantially over the years since the first edition of this book was published in 1990. This brief guide is not intended to be complete and inclusive but it does aim to offer some pointers to further reading in the field.

Steve de Shazer remains adamant that solution focused brief therapy is not a theory. Rather, he states, it is a description of a way of talking with clients. However, the works that most clearly lay out the thinking associated with the approach are his. *Keys to Solution in Brief Therapy* (1985) is the book that de Shazer wrote almost at the birth of solution focused brief therapy, showing both the path of the future and some of the remains of his earlier, more problem-focused way of thinking. *Clues: Investigating Solutions in Brief Therapy* (1988) is his clearest representation of the model, while *Putting Difference to Work* (1991) began to introduce a philosophical and linguistic approach to the model that was more fully developed in *Words were Originally Magic* (1994). Both books highlight the influence on his thinking of Wittgenstein's later philosophical writings, and also include lengthy transcripts of client work that illustrate the model in detail.

There are some books that can be thought of as manuals or workbooks, guiding the reader through a step-by-step exploration of the approach. Much of the writing of Insoo Kim Berg (co-director, with her partner Steve de Shazer, of the Milwaukee Brief Family Therapy Center) is constructed this way. *Interviewing for Solutions*, written jointly with Peter DeJong (1997), is a good example of this type of book, and *Becoming Solution Focused in Brief Therapy* by Walter and Peller (1992) is another.

There is currently just one handbook, *Handbook of Solution-Focused Brief Therapy* edited by Miller, Hubble and Duncan (1996). This large volume includes articles that focus on thinking, on technique and on areas of application as well as looking at some of the research under-pinning the approach. A further supplement to the thinking behind the approach is *A Brief Guide to Brief Therapy* (Cade and O'Hanlon, 1993) which places solution focused brief therapy within a wider context and helps the reader to see its place within a tradition.

Given de Shazer's often repeated assertion that solution focused brief therapy is 'the same', whatever problem the client brings, it is somewhat ironic that there has been a plethora of specific application texts. With the wide use of solution focused brief therapy in the field of alcohol and drugs, it is worth highlighting Insoo Kim Berg and Scott Miller's (1992) book *Working with the Problem Drinker: A solution focused approach* and Insoo Kim Berg and Norman Reuss's (1997) book *Solutions Step by Step: a substance abuse treatment manual*. Yvonne Dolan's work (1991 and 1998) is important for a different reason. She has focused throughout her career on working with survivors of sexual abuse. Her books make the most convincing case for the possibility of using solution focused brief therapy in an area of work that many people instinctively assume not to be appropriate for a solution focus. *Even From A Broken Web*, by O'Hanlon and Bertolino (1998) also focuses on work with survivors of abuse. Barbara McFarland's *Brief Therapy and Eating Disorders* (1995), addresses an area similarly thought to be 'intractable'. Solution focused brief therapy in schools has been covered by several authors, including Rhodes and Ajmal (1995) and Durrant (1995) while Insoo Kim Berg has looked at work within child protection services in her *Family Preservation: A brief therapy workbook* (1991), and again, and covering some of the same material, in *Family Based Services: A solution-focused approach* (1994). Work with couples is the focus of Hudson and O'Hanlon's *Re-writing Love Stories: Brief marital therapy* (1991) and is also the subject of Michelle Weiner-Davis's popular self-help book *Divorce Busting: A revolutionary and rapid program for staying together* (1992). Jane Lethem's book *Moved to Tears, Moved to Action: Brief therapy with women and children* (1994) particularly examines the use of solution focused brief therapy by women working with women and children. Matthew Selekman has published two books on working with children and adolescents (1993 and 1997).

Solution focus has also spawned its own crop of self-help books. Michelle Weiner-Davis has written the modestly entitled *Change your life and everyone in it* (1996) in addition to her earlier book *Divorce Busting*. Miller and Berg (1995) have produced a version of their *Working with the Problem Drinker* for clients, titled *The Miracle Method*. In the same way Hudson and O'Hanlon have translated their book on marriage and relationships into *Stop Blaming, Start Loving! A solution oriented approach to improving your relationship* (1996). It is worth adding that Dolan's (1998) book *One small step* was written for clients, although it is also very helpful for professionals. Two final books in this category are Linda Metcalf's (1997) book *Parenting towards solutions*, and Pat Hudson's (1996) *The Solution Focused Woman – Creating the life you want*.

There are three further texts that are interesting because they pick up solution focused brief therapy in slightly different ways. The first two, Durrant (1993) and Metcalf (1998), look at the application in two specific contexts; Durrant in residential work and Metcalf in group therapy. The third book is quite different from all the others. Miller (1997) in his book *Becoming Miracle Workers: Language and meaning in brief therapy* writes from the perspective of a sociologist examining the development of solution focused brief therapy on the basis of thirteen years' of observation of de Shazer and the team at the Brief Family Therapy Center in Milwaukee. His work focuses on the development of a model, of an approach that within the period of his study has become widely influential throughout the world.

And finally for UK- based readers in particular it might be worth mentioning that there are two further introductory texts written by therapists practicing in England. O'Connell (1998) brings to his book his wide experience in the field of counseling, while Hawkes, Marsh and Wilgosh (1998) draw on their specific expertise in the field of mental health.

EPILOGUE

Solution focused brief therapy is not the new miracle cure. It does not work 100% of the time. Indeed, many other approaches would claim outcomes as good as solution focused brief therapy, and most approaches are in fact relatively brief, if only by default.

On what grounds therefore should you decide whether or not to base your work on solution focused thinking? Consider these four questions. Does the way of thinking about clients that is implied within solution focus fit with your preferred way of thinking about clients? Are the sort of conversations that the approach favours the sort of conversations you would want to have with the people with whom you work? Is the minimally hierarchical, non-expert position which solution focus adopts one with which you would feel comfortable? And, of course, what do you think your clients would make of the work?

If you decide that solution focus could be for you, there is one last thing you should bear in mind. The way that you work tends to have an effect on the rest of your life. What would you do with all the energy that solution focus could release? Could you deal with the sense of optimism that the approach tends to engender?

We hope that reading this book will be of use to you and will make a positive difference to your work with your clients. And if not, that at least you have enjoyed it. Thank you for having reached this far.

REFERENCES

Bateson, G. (1972) *Steps to an Ecology of Mind*. New York: Ballantine Books.

Berg, I. K. (1991) *Family Preservation: A brief therapy workbook*. (ed. George, Evan) London: BT Press.

Berg, I. K. (1994) *Family Based Services: A solution-focused approach*. New York: Norton.

Berg, I. K. and Miller, S.(1992) *Working with the Problem Drinker: A solution focused approach*. New York: Norton.

Berg, I. K. and Reuss, N. (1997) *Solutions Step by Step: a substance abuse treatment manual*. New York: Norton & Wylie.

Cade, B. and O'Hanlon, B.(1993) *A Brief Guide to Brief Therapy*. New York: Norton.

Cecchin, G. (1987) Hypothesising, Circularity and Neutrality Revisited: An Invitation to Curiosity *Family Process* 26:405-413.

De Jong, P. and Berg, I. K. (1997) *Interviewing for Solutions*. Pacific Grove: Brooks/Cole.

De Jong, P. and Hopwood, L.(1996) From the home of solution-focused therapy: outcome research on treatment conducted at the Brief Family Therapy Center, 1992-93, in Miller S., Hubble, M., and Duncan, B. (Eds) *Handbook of Solution Focused Therapy*. San Francisco: Jossey-Bass.

de Shazer, S., Berg, I. K., Lipchik, E., Nunnally, E., Molnar, A., Gingerich, W., Weiner-Davis, M. (1986) Brief Therapy: Focused Solution Development *Family Process* 25:207-222.

de Shazer, S. (1985) *Keys to Solution in Brief Therapy*. New York: Norton.

de Shazer, S. (1988) *Clues: Investigating Solutions in Brief Therapy* New York: Norton.

de Shazer, S. (1991) *Putting Difference to Work*. New York: Norton.

de Shazer, S. (1994) *Words Were Originally Magic*. New York: Norton.

Dolan, Y. (1991) *Resolving Sexual Abuse*. New York: Norton.

Dolan, Y. (1998) *One Small Step: Moving beyond trauma and therapy to a life of joy*. London: BT Press.

Durrant, M. (1995) *Creative Strategies for School Problems*. New York: Norton.

Durrant, M.(1993) *Residential treatment*. New York: Norton.

Gingerich, W., de Shazer, S. and Weiner-Davis, M. (1987) Constructing Change: A Research View of Interviewing, in Lipchik, E. (ed.) *Interviewing* Rockville: Aspen.

Hawkes, D., Marsh, I., and Wilgosh, R. (1998) *Solution Focused Therapy: A handbook for health care professionals*. Oxford: Butterworth Heinemann.

Hoffman, L. (1990) Constructing Realities: An Art of Lenses *Family Process* 29:1-12.

Hudson, P. (1996) *The Solution Focused Woman – Creating the life you want*. New York Norton.

Hudson, Patricia O'Hanlon and O'Hanlon, William Hudson (1991) *Re-writing Love Stories: brief marital therapy*. New York: Norton.

Hudson, Patricia O'Hanlon and O'Hanlon, William Hudson (1996) *Stop blaming, start loving – a solution orientated approach to improving your relationship*. New York: Norton.

Iveson, C. (1996) Solution Focused Brief Therapy: Working with young people, in Sigston, A., Curran, P., Labram, A., Wolfendale, S. (Eds) *Psychology in Practice with Young People, Families and Schools*. London: David Fulton.

Iveson, D. (1991) (Unpublished) Institute of Family Therapy/Birkbeck College.

Kral, R. and Kowalski, K. (1989) After the Miracle: The Second Stage in Solution-Focused Brief Therapy, *Journal of Strategic and Systemic Therapies* 8:73-76.

Lethem, J. (1994) *Moved to Tears, Moved to Action: Brief therapy with women and children*. London: BT Press

Lipchik, E. and de Shazer, S. (1986) The Purposeful Interview *Journal of Strategic and Systemic Therapies* 5:88-99.

Lipchik, E. (1988) Interviewing with a Constructive Ear, in *Questions in Therapy*, Special Edition, Dulwich Centre Newsletter.

McFarland, B.(1995) *Brief Therapy and Eating Disorders*. SanFrancisco: Jossey-Bass.

Metcalf, L.(1997) *Parenting Towards Solutions: How parents can use skills they already have to raise responsible, loving kids.* Englewood Cliffs, NJ: Prentice Hall, Simon & Schuster.

Metcalf, L. (1998) *Solution Focused Group Therapy.* New York: Simon & Schuster.

Miller, S.and Berg, I. K. (1995) *The Miracle method: A radically new approach to problem drinking.* New York: Norton.

Miller, G. (1998) *Becoming Miracle Workers: Language and meaning in Brief Therapy.* New York: Aldine de Gruyter.

Miller, S. Hubble, M., and Duncan, B.(Eds.) (1996) *Handbook of Solution-Focused Brief Therapy.* San Francisco: Jossey-Bass.

Miller, S., Duncan, B. and Hubble, M. (1997) *Escape from Babel: Towards a unifying language for psychotherapy practice.* New York: Norton.

O'Connell, B. (1998) *Solution-Focused Therapy.* London: Sage.

O'Hanlon, B. and Beadle, S. (1996) *A Field Guide to PossibilityLand.* London: BT Press.

O'Hanlon, B. and Bertolino, B. (1998) *Even from a Broken Web: Brief, respectful solution-oriented therapy for sexual abuse and trauma.* New York: Wiley.

O'Hanlon, B. and Hexum, A. (1990) *An Uncommon Casebook: The complete clinical work of Milton H. Erickson* New York: Norton.

O'Hanlon, W. and Weiner-Davis, M. (1989) *In Search of Solutions* New York: Norton.

Ratner, H. (1998) Solution Focused Brief Therapy: From hierarchy to collaboration, in Bayne, R., Nicolson, P., Horton, I. (Eds) *Counselling and Communication Skills for Medical and Health Practitioners.* Leicester: BPS.

Ratner, H. and Yandoli, D. (1996) Solution Focused Brief Therapy: A co-operative approach to work with clients, in Edwards, G., Dare, C. (Eds) *Psychotherapy, Psychological Treatments and the Addictions.* Cambridge: CUP.

Rhodes, J. and Ajmal, Y. (1995) *Solution Focused Thinking in Schools.* London: BT Press.

Selekman, M. (1993) *Pathways to Change: Brief therapy solutions with difficult adolescents.* New York: Guilford Press.

Selekman, M. (1997) *Solution Focused Therapy with Children.* New York:

Guilford Press.

Walter, J. and Peller, J. (1992) *Becoming Solution-Focused in Brief Therapy*. New York: Brunner/Mazel.

Weiner-Davis, M. (1992) *Divorce Busting: A revolutionary and rapid program for staying together*. New York: Simon & Schuster.

Weiner-Davis, M., (1996) *Change your life and everyone in it*. New York: Fireside.

Weiner-Davis, M., de Shazer, S., Gingerich, W.J. (1987) Building on Pre-Treatment Change to Construct the Therapeutic Solution: An Exploratory Study, *Journal of Marital and Family Therapy* 13:359-365.

White, M. (1991) Deconstruction and Therapy, in *Postmodernism, Deconstruction and Therapy*. Dulwich Centre Newsletter.

White, M. and Epston, D. (1990) *Narrative Means to Therapeutic Ends*. New York: Norton.